I0047522

Entrepreneurship Education and Training

A WORLD BANK STUDY

Entrepreneurship Education and Training

Insights from Ghana, Kenya, and Mozambique

Alicia Robb, Alexandria Valerio, and Brent Parton, Editors

THE WORLD BANK
Washington, D.C.

© 2014 International Bank for Reconstruction and Development / The World Bank
1818 H Street NW, Washington, DC 20433
Telephone: 202-473-1000; Internet: www.worldbank.org

Some rights reserved

1 2 3 4 17 16 15 14

World Bank Studies are published to communicate the results of the Bank's work to the development community with the least possible delay. The manuscript of this paper therefore has not been prepared in accordance with the procedures appropriate to formally edited texts.

This work is a product of the staff of The World Bank with external contributions. The findings, interpretations, and conclusions expressed in this work do not necessarily reflect the views of The World Bank, its Board of Executive Directors, or the governments they represent. The World Bank does not guarantee the accuracy of the data included in this work. The boundaries, colors, denominations, and other information shown on any map in this work do not imply any judgment on the part of The World Bank concerning the legal status of any territory or the endorsement or acceptance of such boundaries.

Nothing herein shall constitute or be considered to be a limitation upon or waiver of the privileges and immunities of The World Bank, all of which are specifically reserved.

Rights and Permissions

This work is available under the Creative Commons Attribution 3.0 IGO license (CC BY 3.0 IGO) http://creativecommons.org/licenses/by/3.0/igo. Under the Creative Commons Attribution license, you are free to copy, distribute, transmit, and adapt this work, including for commercial purposes, under the following conditions:

Attribution—Please cite the work as follows: Robb, Alicia, Alexandria Valerio, and Brent Parton, eds. 2014. *Entrepreneurship Education and Training: Insights from Ghana, Kenya, and Mozambique.* World Bank Studies. Washington, DC: World Bank. doi:10.1596/978-1-4648-0278-2. License: Creative Commons Attribution CC BY 3.0 IGO

Translations—If you create a translation of this work, please add the following disclaimer along with the attribution: *This translation was not created by The World Bank and should not be considered an official World Bank translation. The World Bank shall not be liable for any content or error in this translation.*

Adaptations—If you create an adaptation of this work, please add the following disclaimer along with the attribution: *This is an adaptation of an original work by The World Bank. Responsibility for the views and opinions expressed in the adaptation rests solely with the author or authors of the adaptation and are not endorsed by The World Bank.*

Third-party content—The World Bank does not necessarily own each component of the content contained within the work. The World Bank therefore does not warrant that the use of any third-party-owned individual component or part contained in the work will not infringe on the rights of those third parties. The risk of claims resulting from such infringement rests solely with you. If you wish to re-use a component of the work, it is your responsibility to determine whether permission is needed for that re-use and to obtain permission from the copyright owner. Examples of components can include, but are not limited to, tables, figures, or images.

All queries on rights and licenses should be addressed to the Publishing and Knowledge Division, The World Bank, 1818 H Street NW, Washington, DC 20433, USA; fax: 202-522-2625; e-mail: pubrights@worldbank.org.

ISBN (paper): 978-1-4648-0278-2
ISBN (electronic): 978-1-4648-0279-9
DOI: 10.1596/978-1-4648-0278-2

Cover photo: © Marie McCarthy. Used with the permission of Marie McCarthy. Further permission required for reuse.
Cover design: Debra Naylor, Naylor Design.

Library of Congress Cataloging-in-Publication Data has been requested.

Contents

Acknowledgments

This report was prepared by a team led by Alexandria Valerio (World Bank) and composed of Alicia Robb (Kauffman Foundation and University of California, Berkeley) and Brent Parton (World Bank). Sebastian Monroy-Taborda (World Bank) provided overall research support. The report summarizes the findings from country case studies undertaken in three countries in Sub-Saharan Africa: Ghana, Kenya, and Mozambique. Fieldwork activities were coordinated by World Bank task team leaders including Peter Darvas (Ghana), Helen Craig (Kenya), and Ana Ruth Menezes (Mozambique). The research teams responsible for preparing the case studies included Akua Ofori-Ampofo, Wilberforce Owusu-Ansah (KNUST), and Kofi Poku in Ghana; Jutta Franz, Wairimu Kiambuthi, and David Muthaka (Kenya Institute for Public Policy Research and Analysis) in Kenya; and Constantino Marrengula, Zeferino Martins, and Manolo Sanchez in Mozambique.

Helpful peer review and general comments were provided on an early version of the case studies by the following World Bank colleagues: Louise Fox, Margo Hoftijzer, Mattias Lundberg, Maria Paulina Mogollon, and Michel Welmond. The team expresses appreciation to all individuals who participated in one-on-one interviews or focus groups in the cities of Malindi, Mombasa, and Nairobi in Kenya; Accra and Kumasi in Ghana; and Manica, Maputo, and Nampula in Mozambique; and Michael Freese (Professor, National University of Singapore) and Bob Nelson (Professor Emeritus, College of Education, University of Illinois), who generously shared their time and technical expertise with the team.

The team is also thankful for the overall assistance received from Elise Egoume-Bossogo, Lorelei Lacdao, and Marie Madeleine Ndaw. The written pieces of this study were edited by Marc DeFrancis (DeFrancis Writing & Editing).

Finally, the team appreciates the leadership and technical support of Elizabeth King (Sector Director, Human Development Network) and Harry Patrinos (Sector Manager, Human Development Network) of the World Bank.

The report received financial support from the Bank-Netherlands Partnership Program with the World Bank.

About the Editors

Alicia Robb is a senior fellow with the Kauffman Foundation. She is also a visiting scholar at the University of California, Berkeley; the Basque Institute for Competitiveness in San Sebastian, Spain; and the Federal Reserve Bank of Atlanta. She is the founder and past executive director and board chair of the Foundation for Sustainable Development, an international development organization working in Africa, India, and Latin America (www.fsdinternational.org). Alicia received her MS and PhD in economics from the University of North Carolina at Chapel Hill. She has previously worked with the Office of Economic Research in the Small Business Administration and the Federal Reserve Board of Governors. She is also a prolific author on the topic of entrepreneurship. In addition to authoring numerous journal articles and book chapters, she is the coauthor of *Race and Entrepreneurial Success*, published by MIT Press, and *A Rising Tide: Financing Strategies for Women-Owned Businesses*, published by Stanford University Press. She serves on the board of the National Advisory Council for Minority Business Enterprise and on the advisory board for Global Entrepreneurship Week, and she is a guest contributor to outlets such as The Huffington Post and *Forbes*.

Alexandria Valerio is a senior economist in the Education Department at the World Bank. Alexandria currently leads global research agendas focused on identifying the characteristics of effective entrepreneurship education and training programs and implementing large-scale surveys to measure skills sets of adults and their impact on a range of outcomes. Before joining the Education Department, she led the policy dialogue and project portfolios in Argentina, Brazil, Chile, Nicaragua, Panama, and Paraguay in the Latin America and the Caribbean region; and Angola and Mozambique in the Africa region. Her published work includes peer-reviewed papers on the cost and financing of early childhood development, impacts of school fees, technical vocational education and training, workforce development, and school-based health programs. She holds a PhD in comparative and international education from Columbia University and a master's in public administration from the Maxwell School of Citizenship and Public Affairs at Syracuse University.

Brent Parton is an education consultant for the World Bank. He has research, technical, and writing experience across a range of education, workforce, and health issues. With the World Bank, in addition to his work on the linkages among entrepreneurship, education, and economic development, he supported a global program benchmarking workforce development systems and a research project investigating the political economy of education reform in developing countries. He holds an MEd in international education policy and management and a BA in history, both from Vanderbilt University.

Abbreviations

ABET	Adult Basic Education and Training
ACWICT	African Center for Women, Information and Communications Technology
ADB	African Development Bank
AIDS	acquired immune deficiency syndrome
AIMO	All India Manufacturers' Organisation
APSB	Auchi Polytechnic School of Business
BEDEC	Business & Entrepreneur Development Centre
BNPP	Bank-Netherlands Partnership Program
BSMDP	Business Service Market Development Project
CADI	Industrial Development Advisory Centre
CEED	Centre for Entrepreneurship & Enterprise Development
CEM	Certificate in Entrepreneurial Management
CET	Creative Enterprise Training
EE	entrepreneurship education
EEHE	entrepreneurship education programs in higher education
EESE	entrepreneurship education for secondary education students
EET	entrepreneurial education and training
END	Endeavor
EPAG	Economic Empowerment of Adolescent Girls and Young Women
ET	entrepreneurship training
ETPo	entrepreneurship training for potential entrepreneurs
ETPr	entrepreneurship training for practicing entrepreneurs
FBO	farm-based organization
GDP	gross domestic product
GEDI	Global Entrepreneurship Development Index
GEM	Global Entrepreneurship Monitor

GNAG	Ghana National Association of Garages
GOWE	Growth-Oriented Women Entrepreneurs
GYEEDA	Ghana Youth Enterprise and Entrepreneurial Development Agency
HDNSP	Human Development Network Social Protection
HIV	human immunodeficiency virus
IAC	Chimoio Agricultural Institute
IFC	International Finance Corporation
ILO	International Labour Organization
IPEME	Institute for Promotion of Small and Medium-Sized Enterprises
IPEX	Institute for Export Promotion
IRD	International Relief and Development
JAN	Junior Achievement Namibia
KAB	Know About Business
KAWBO	Kenya Association of Women Business Owners
KIBT	Kenya Institute of Business Training
KNBS	Kenya National Bureau of Statistics
KNUST	Kwame Nkrumah University of Science and Tech
KYBT	Kenya Youth Business Trust
KYEEI	Kenya Youth Empowerment and Employment Initiative
KYEP	Kenya Youth Empowerment Program
LESDEP	Local Enterprises and Skill Development
MEST	Meltwater Entrepreneurial School of Technology
MiDA-FBO	Millennium Development Authority—Farm-Based Organization Training
MIT AITI	Massachusetts Institute of Technology Accelerating Information Technology Innovation
MoHEST	Ministry of Higher Education, Science and Technology
MSE	micro- and small-scale enterprises
MSETTP	Micro and Small Enterprise Training and Technology Project
OIC	Opportunities Industrialization Centers
OVOP	One Village One Product
PACDE	Support to Competitiveness and Enterprise Development Project
PIREP	Program to Reform Technical and Vocational Education and Training
PRES	Economic Rehabilitation Program

PRIDE	Promotion of Rural Initiative and Development Enterprises Limited
RIC	Research and Incubation Center
SAIE	South African Institute for Entrepreneurship
SCORE	Sustaining Competitive and Responsible Enterprises
SME	small and medium enterprises
SMIDO	Suame Magazine Industrial Development Organization
SNV	Stichting Nederlandse Vrijwilligers (Netherlands Development Organization)
STEP	Student Training for Entrepreneurship Promotion
STIFIMO	Science, Technology and Innovation between Finland and Mozambique
STRYDE	Strengthening Rural Youth Development through Enterprise
TIVET	technical and vocational education and training
UNIDO	United Nations Industrial Development Organization
UPSA	University of Professional Studies Accra
USAID	U.S. Agency for International Development
WEP	Women's Entrepreneurship Program
WINGS	Women's Income Generating Support
YEDF	Young Enterprise Development Fund
YOP	Youth Opportunities Program

Executive Summary

Relevance

Governments around the world have shown a growing interest in interventions that promote entrepreneurial success, making significant investments in entrepreneurial education and training (EET). This is happening not only in developed nations, but also across the developing world as well. Empirical research has found positive correlations not only between entrepreneurial activity and innovation, but also between entrepreneurship and job creation. Skilled entrepreneurship offers potential rewards for individuals across the socioeconomic spectrum, including vulnerable populations and workers in the informal sector for whom it signifies potentially more stable income flows, increased profits, and more secure employment.

The question remains, however, whether entrepreneurial success can be taught and, if so, what is the best way to teach it. Preliminary research has reached mixed conclusions across a range of outcomes associated with EET programs. Furthermore, findings are mixed regarding the extent to which programs are able support various individuals, from poor and vulnerable groups to educated aspiring entrepreneurs with significant work experience. Findings are further complicated by the fact that training and education programs are delivered in heterogeneous cultural and educational contexts. Yet, despite thin evidence, and in particular a lack of information on outcomes and costs, the global EET experiment continues.

The effectiveness of EET may prove especially important to the three case study countries examined in this study. Ghana, Kenya, and Mozambique are all experiencing sustained economic growth, increased foreign direct investment, and diversification in their private sectors, and in all three countries the less-capital-intensive service sector is becoming increasingly important. These facts, combined with the presence of massive informal sectors of self-employed workers, make these economies fertile ground for taking entrepreneurship to the next level.

Understanding what is and what is not working in the EET field also matters from a policy standpoint. The business climate in all three countries continues to face severe barriers—from unfriendly regulatory burdens and limited financing to corruption and limited infrastructure. Thus, it remains critical to find out which failures in small business growth stem from these environmental pressures and which stem from a relative lack of basic business skills and entrepreneurial mind-set. To do so, a necessary first step is to understand the elements in EET programming.

The findings of this study, which draw on both global and country-specific research, as well as on the experience of practicing entrepreneurs and students of entrepreneurship in the countries studied, help map out EET practices in these countries and, by extension, in Sub-Saharan Africa in a variety of contexts.

The Knowledge Challenge, and What This Study Addresses

The sheer heterogeneity of EET programs and the complexity involved in tying them to their variety of associated outcomes can muddle policymakers' and practitioners' picture of what is working. The challenge here is considerable.

The body of research on effectiveness remains limited, and much of it is methodologically weak. While some research indicates that programs can improve knowledge, global EET research is unable to draw a direct causal link connecting the enhanced knowledge with the subsequent performance of enterprises. In the case countries, little follow-up research has been carried out to test the effectiveness of programs, including large-scale programs such as Kenya's nationwide public school curriculum. Outside the case countries, a few studies have shown a significant positive relationship between business success and investment in human capital development, and specific EET programs have demonstrated great promise. However, much more fine-grained analysis needs to be done, particularly with regard to the validity of EET as an antipoverty intervention as well as its direct connection to improving business performance in terms of enhanced profits and prospects for firm growth.

The case studies summarized in this report are designed to inform a broader understanding of how EET programs are being designed in these countries, whom they are targeting, and what needs they have been established to help meet. The study also reviews the specific barriers to entrepreneurship that prevail in each country, based on interviews with practicing entrepreneurs, and examines the extent to which the programs are addressing those barriers.

Consequently, the study is able to identify practical insights into current EET program design and implementation that are relevant to various target groups, intended outcomes, and social and economic contexts. While it cannot fill the serious knowledge gap in measurements of program effectiveness, it does supply stakeholder perspectives that often hint strongly at what works best. Overall, the study paints a comprehensive picture of both the context for entrepreneurship and the landscape of programs in the case countries, framing them within the economic, political, and cultural trends that are the dynamic environment within which they have originated and have been evolving. It also lines up these findings against the knowledge we have of programs being implemented around the world.

Key Findings

Key macroeconomic trends give reason for optimism about the trajectory of private sector development, while steep and widespread barriers to entrepreneurship also remain. All three case countries have been on strong growth trajectories, Ghana now ranking among the 10 fastest-growing economies in the world. In each country, prospects for export-driven growth are significant and the growing service sector makes up roughly 50 percent of GDP. However, barriers abound. The labor market itself poses a problem, as all three countries suffer from very high youth unemployment. That in turn helps fuel the growth of necessity-driven entrepreneurship and, therefore, of the informal economy, which in Kenya accounts for 86 percent of *all* new jobs. This last fact might also signify an opportunity for EET, since it implies a vast population of enterprising individuals who should have much to gain from formalizing their businesses.

At the same time, both global monitoring studies and the entrepreneurs interviewed for this study report that corruption, prohibitively high taxes, and burdensome regulatory regimes remain serious impediments to business ownership. Crime and insecurity also remain a very large concern, especially for those in the informal sector. In addition to those barriers, the two impediments mentioned most often by entrepreneurs in the study are cultural disincentives, for example discouragement by family and peers, and lack of access to finance.

The EET landscape is populated by a variety of programs designed to reach a variety of different populations, and their goals vary just as widely. EET programs often emerge as responses to key contextual challenges, a striking example being Mozambique's national program that originally targeted demobilized soldiers when its civil war ended. Other programs target secondary students, a prime example being Kenya's entrepreneurship curriculum, which has been mainstreamed in schools since the 1990s. Still other programs target higher education students, sometimes as stand-alone degree programs and in many cases targeting high-growth-potential candidates such as high-tech students. At another extreme are a large number of programs that target the most vulnerable, such as rural women or unemployed urban youth.

With such diverse target audiences, these EET programs naturally vary in their emphasis. In all three countries, programs targeting vulnerable potential entrepreneurs often have poverty reduction as their goal rather than skill acquisition per se. Those focused on youth often make job acquisition a priority. Secondary school EET programs, by contrast, are more likely to devote energy to developing a broad understanding of business principles.

EET programs are insufficiently tailored to their participants' backgrounds and needs, and they suffer from lack of coordination and information sharing. Despite the program diversity just described, too many EET programs fail to tailor their curriculum and methods to their audience and its needs. The stakeholders interviewed suggested that many programs, especially large programs designed to address youth unemployment, mix large, heterogeneous groups of participants of varying ages, educational backgrounds, experience, and expectations, resulting in mismatches between content and needs. This finding suggests that the program landscape in the case countries may benefit from a more tiered understanding of how different types of EET programs can benefit various groups. For the broader interventions, an emphasis is needed on building foundational skills and mind-sets. For focused interventions, program objectives, for example whether a program is aiming to promote either necessity-driven or high-growth-potential practicing entrepreneurs, should drive program design. On a related note, there is a need for more dialogue among EET programs and operators, not only to avoid duplication and the inefficient use of resources, but also to promote cross-program learning regarding emerging practices.

Stakeholders believe the development of business acumen and an entrepreneurial mind-set are keys to success, though few EET programs focus on these elements. Unanimously, the practicing and potential entrepreneurs interviewed mentioned these skill areas as the most important determinants of success in business. Many also pointed to negative cultural biases, such as family pressure to avoid risk-taking, as barriers; they felt strongly that exposure to entrepreneurial thinking at an early age is key to overcoming them. In both Kenya and Ghana, most EET participants believe that their programs are good at teaching critical general business and financial skills but less effective in developing entrepreneurial attitudes, problem solving skills, and soft skills generally.

Stakeholders need greater exposure to the business community and access to finance, though few EET programs address these needs. EET stakeholders across the case countries indicate a desire for greater exposure to the business community and practicing entrepreneurs. Despite this desire, very few identified programs prioritize such exposure. Available evaluations of programs outside these countries that combine grants with activities such as internships and mentoring services show that they do have more impact than simple training programs.

Stakeholders also cited lack of access to finance as a major problem. Very few EET programs in the case countries provide wrap-around or follow-up services to help remedy this. Nevertheless, a notable trend is the involvement of business associations in providing training for practicing entrepreneurs in their fields; global research suggests that such programs result in improved access to loans for their participants, although whether this stems from the training itself or from affiliation with sponsoring banks remains unclear. The involvement of business associations, and other less direct forms of support for EET may be instructive for policymakers, particularly in the context of supporting potential high growth entrepreneurs.

Going Forward

These findings and the others in this study should be very useful in filling some of the critical knowledge gaps that have made it difficult to know what is being taught, to whom, and with what general effect. They point to—although they do not yet demonstrate conclusively—specific characteristics of EET programs that contribute to the promotion of entrepreneurial attitudes, the attainment of entrepreneurial skills, and the improvement of entrepreneurial outcomes. Finally, the findings in this report can inform EET policy and program dialogue at multiple levels, guide the investment decisions that policymakers and government institutions must make with regard to EET programs, and more clearly indicate in which direction further research in the EET realm is most needed.

CHAPTER 1

Introduction

There is a growing interest in the role that entrepreneurship can play as a catalyst to achieve a number of economic and social development objectives (Brock and Evans 1989; Acs 1992; Carree and Thurik 2003; Volkmann 2009; Bandiera et al. 2012). Empirical studies find positive correlations between entrepreneurial activity, innovation, and technological change (Acs and Varga 2005; Van Praag and Versloot 2007). Furthermore, entrepreneurship is a critical driver of job creation (Birch 1979), either through self-employment growth or as suppliers to the corporate sectors (Fritsch 2004; Acs and Armington 2006; Schramm and Litan 2009). In addition, entrepreneurship is often looked to as a mechanism for achieving stable income flows and increased profits (Hermes and Lensink 2007; Karlan and Valdivia 2011), particularly for SME owners, including workers in the informal sector and vulnerable populations.

Given the potential beneficial spillovers of entrepreneurship, governments around the world have taken an interest in interventions that promote and facilitate entrepreneurial success through required support systems and the removal of barriers to entrepreneurship (McKernan 2002; Paulson and Townsend 2004; DeMel, McKenzie, and Woodruff 2009). These promotion efforts include the easing of business environment constraints, the enhancement of access to finance and credit, and the provision of support to strengthen business practices and enterprise management.

About Entrepreneurship Education and Training

One subset of the larger portfolio of entrepreneurial promotion programs consists of entrepreneurship education and entrepreneurship training (EET) programs. These are programs that seek to develop the attitudes, knowledge, and skills associated with the practice of entrepreneurship. They are based on research indicating that some entrepreneurial behaviors can be taught and learned, starting in people's youth and culminating in their young adult or adult years or when they are potential or practicing entrepreneurs (Hegarty 2006; Souitaris, Zerbinati, and Al-Laham 2007; Walter and Dohse 2009).

EET itself encompasses a heterogeneous array of programs, including formal academic education programs and stand-alone training programs. Both of the latter may aim to stimulate entrepreneurship as well as support individuals and enterprises already engaged in entrepreneurial activities. These interventions can target a range of individuals and have a variety of program objectives, from enhancing socio-emotional skills (such as locus of control and self-confidence) among secondary education students, to teaching business plan development to graduate students, to providing training in bookkeeping to subsistence farmers. The diversity of these interventions reflects the variety of those who can be considered "entrepreneurs."

Despite global interest in EET, the body of available research remains limited, and what exists to date tends to be methodologically weak (Glaub and Frese 2011). However, EET is a growing area of interest for a number of researchers, and a set of existing evaluations demonstrate mixed but promising results (van der Sluis, van Praag, and Vijverberg 2005; Lautenschläger and Haase 2011; Unger et al. 2011). Further complicating the picture of EET effectiveness is the fact that most EET evaluations examine a range of outcomes. For example, a recent meta-analysis by McKenzie and Woodruff (2012) demonstrates relatively modest impacts of training on the survivorship of existing firms, but few significant impacts on profits or sales. A meta-analysis by Cho and Honorati (2013) indicates that while programs can improve knowledge, this does not necessarily lead to related gains in performance and status outcomes.

Several meta-analyses, however, give more weight to the promise of EET programs to enhance trainees' entrepreneurial capabilities (knowledge and skills) by shedding light on how these capabilities may ultimately contribute to better entrepreneurial performance. A meta-analysis by Unger and others (2011) finds a significant positive relationship between success (size, profitability, and growth) and the mere investment in human capital development. Furthermore, in that study the positive effects on success of the skills and knowledge resulting from those investments are even stronger than the investments alone and stronger still for knowledge and skills specifically related to entrepreneurship. Another meta-analysis, Martin, McNally, and Kay (2013) find significant relationships among EET, entrepreneurship-related human capital assets (entrepreneurial knowledge and skill, positive perception of entrepreneurship, and intentions to start a business), and entrepreneurship outcomes (nascent behaviors, start-up behaviors, and financial success). They further find differential effects between academic-focused and training-focused EET interventions, with stronger effects associated with the former type of EET.

The sheer heterogeneity of EET programs and the complexity involved in tying them to their variety of associated outcomes can muddle policymakers' and practitioners' picture of what is working and what is not. Acknowledging the need for more evidence to rigorously link EET programs to desired outcomes around entrepreneurial activity or success, policymakers and practitioners will likely be interested in the experience of others in developing and implementing EET programs across a variety of contexts. In turn, focused, qualitative investigations into EET programs may also bring critical insights to bear for the design and implementation of future EET programs that aim at particular beneficiaries, or to engender particular outcomes, or within particular contexts.

About the Case Studies

Complementing Global EET Research

This chapter summarizes the findings from three case studies that examine EET programs across three Sub-Saharan African countries: Ghana, Kenya, and Mozambique. The case studies are a follow-on research component of a broader research effort on global EET programs, *Entrepreneurship Education and Training Programs Around the World: Dimensions for Success* (Valerio, Parton, and Robb 2014). The research effort identifies and catalogs the range of EET program types as well as the program dimensions that shape program outcomes, presents a Conceptual Framework for EET, and presents an analysis of both EET research and a global sample of program evaluations. Building on the observations of that analysis, the present report describes a set of practical insights about EET program design and implementation across target groups, intended outcomes, and contexts.

The importance of this topic is reflected within the World Bank's Education Sector Strategy 2020, "Learning for All: Investing in People's Knowledge and Skills to Promote Development" (World Bank 2011b) and responds directly to Step Four of the Skills Toward Employment and Productivity Framework. With regard to the broader employment picture in Sub-Saharan Africa, this work complements the World Bank's recent report on "Youth Employment in Sub-Saharan Africa" (Filmer et al. 2014). Specifically, this study corresponds to the goal of encouraging entrepreneurship and innovation (World Bank 2010a). It aligns with the Bank's Social Protection and Labor Strategy 2012–22, "Resilience, Equity and Opportunity" (World Bank 2012b), and it complements a new multi-sector work program being led by the Bank's Social Protection Network (HDNSP), "Supporting Self-Employment and Small-Scale Entrepreneurship: Creating and Improving Alternatives to Wage Employment." It builds upon the existing multi-sector effort that examines the broader population of entrepreneurship promotion programs, including but not limited to EET, which is financed by a Trust Fund from the Bank-Netherlands Partnership Program (BNPP).

Objective of the Case Studies

The summary of the case studies presented here provide important information to improve our understanding of EET in three Sub-Saharan African countries. Each country has its unique challenges and opportunities, as well as unique cultural contexts, relevant to EET. The primary objective of the studies is to complement the broader research effort by providing targeted, qualitative insights into the landscape of EET programs in these countries. A key question each case study seeks to answer is the extent to which the programs address the country's

relevant barriers to entrepreneurship. Each case study was thus designed to provide a comprehensive picture of both the context for entrepreneurship and the
landscape of programs in the country, in order to understand how these programs
are structured, what they aim to achieve, and how they relate to one other as well
as to other programs being implemented around the world. Further, each case
study aims to capture the program insights local EET stakeholders have in order
to better understand how programs are meeting—or can better meet—their
needs.

Producing the Case Studies

Each case study was structured to illustrate the country's entrepreneurial context, the landscape of EET programs and its relationship to the entrepreneurial
context, and the perceptions and views of practicing and potential entrepreneurs
as well as EET program managers. First, to sketch a picture of the entrepreneurial
context, desk reviews of available country-level and global research were conducted, and these were subsequently supplemented with insights from interviewees and target groups.

Methods used to identify programs in each country's EET landscape included Internet searches, screening of information from reports and newspaper
articles on business sector and entrepreneurship development, and interviews
with stakeholders. Following the snowball principle, interviews with one identified program led to further information on other programs. During initial
identification, no specific filter was applied. Ultimately, teams identified 111
EET programs in Kenya, 80 programs in Ghana, and 31 programs in
Mozambique. The amount of information available for these programs varied
significantly. Ultimately, these initial program lists were filtered based upon the
amount of information that was available to inform the study. The filtered
program landscapes include 42 EET programs in Ghana (listed in appendix A),
42 programs in Kenya (listed in appendix B), and 27 programs in Mozambique
(listed in appendix C).

In terms of limitations, the strong reliance on information provided through
the Internet during the initial scoping process posed some constraints in the
comprehensiveness and accuracy of the initial information. It fostered some self-
selection in the sense that programs without Internet presence tended to be
excluded, though a few programs without Internet presence were included.
Second, the scope of information provided was not uniform, and often it was
limited in nature. In this regard, a major challenge for the study turned out to be
the low level of monitoring and evaluation of EET programs, which limited the
information available on outcomes.

Finally, since each case study sought to distill lessons for bringing the EET
programs closer to meeting the needs of existing, new, or would-be entrepreneurs, it captured the insights of local EET stakeholders through a series of qualitative surveys, interviews, and focus groups conducted by research teams in each
country. The goal was to gain a better understanding of stakeholders' views on
these questions:

- *What are the characteristics and skills needed to succeed in business ownership?*
- *What constraints and barriers affect the ability of potential and practicing entrepreneurs to start and grow their businesses?*
- *How effective are existing EET programs in meeting the needs of local entrepreneurs?*
- *What policies, programs, and practices are still needed?*

This qualitative fieldwork focused on five target groups: program managers, successful entrepreneurs, failed entrepreneurs, potential entrepreneurs in EET programming, and practicing entrepreneurs in entrepreneurship training (ET) programming. Individual interviews were conducted with program managers and successful entrepreneurs, while focus group discussions were held with potential, practicing, and failed/discouraged entrepreneurs. Interviewees were selected with the goal of achieving broad coverage of both program types and industries. The methodology used to collect data was standard for the three countries (Ghana, Kenya, and Mozambique) using the same instruments to conduct the interviews and focus groups. The instruments were translated into Portuguese by the Mozambican team, and some of the interviews and focus groups were conducted in local languages in Ghana and Kenya as well.

Field teams conducted between 7 and 10 qualitative interviews from each of the 2 target groups (program managers and successful entrepreneurs) for a total of 15 to 20 qualitative interviews. Qualitative interviews were semi-structured (or focused) and included a series of open-ended questions based on specific topic areas. The questions differed, depending on whether the person being interviewed was a program manager/administrator or an entrepreneur as well as on the type of participant the program targeted. Qualitative information was gathered on the individual's feelings, perceptions, and opinions. Field teams conducted 2 to 3 focus groups for each target group with 5 to 7 participants in each group, for a total of 8 focus groups and 40 to 60 participants. Focus groups were also varied, including various industry sectors, types of programs, and target populations. The focus group and qualitative interview instruments can be found in appendixes D, E, F, G, and H. Details on the focus groups and qualitative surveys for each country can be found in appendixes I (Ghana), J (Kenya), and K (Mozambique).

The majority of the fieldwork for the EET case studies was conducted between February and May 2013. Focus groups and interviews were conducted in multiple locations in Ghana (in the cities of Accra and Kumasi), Kenya (Malindi, Mombasa, and Nairobi), and Mozambique (Manica, Maputo, and Nampula). With rare exceptions, the EET programs identified have not been the subject of specific reviews or evaluations that could give an independent assessment of their relevance, effectiveness, and impact. Most do not have built-in monitoring and evaluation systems that would make it possible to assess whether the results corresponded to their stated objectives. Thus, the perceptions of program managers, successful and failed entrepreneurs, and beneficiaries were the only sources of data to assess the quality and effectiveness of the programs. Four different dimensions of EET programs were considered: Program Design and Evaluation; Trainers and Delivery; Content and Curriculum; and Wrap-Around Services. The qualitative surveys and focus groups delved into more detail along these different dimensions and also investigated the nuances that stemmed from country context.

About the Report

This report summarizes the key themes and findings from three in-depth case studies of EET programs in Ghana, Kenya, and Mozambique. Each case study produced rich information on the programs' context, the landscape of programs in each country, and the qualitative insights from local EET stakeholders. This report synthesizes information from across the case studies to analyze the extent to which these countries' programs are meeting the needs of local entrepreneurs. It also introduces findings from global EET research to show how programs in the case-study countries relate to what is known about global practice in EET. From this synthesis, the report presents a set of key findings intended to illuminate how EET programs can be better aligned with local needs and promising EET practices globally.

Structure

The report is structured in six chapters and presents key insights from across the case studies along the way. Chapter 1 is the introduction chapter. Chapter 2 introduces a common framework for EET, drawn from the complementary study, *Entrepreneurship Education and Training Programs Around the World: Dimensions for Success* (Valerio, Parton, and Robb 2014), in order to provide a common definition and language for a discussion of the diverse universe of EET programs. Chapter 3 summarizes the economic, political, and cultural contexts as well as the entrepreneurial environments for EET programs across the case-study countries, drawing upon both existing research and the insights of local EET stakeholders. Chapter 4 summarizes the landscape of programs identified by the case studies according to program type and explores connections with relevant findings from global EET research. Chapter 5 presents a set of key thematic findings from the qualitative fieldwork. Chapter 6 concludes with a summary of the cross-cutting findings from the case studies and insights into the implications for policymakers and program designers.

Usefulness

This report seeks to provide operational and technical lessons that can be used to inform the design and implementation of existing or new EET programs, both within the countries studied and beyond. The findings also help to fill a critical knowledge gap in the specific characteristics of EET programs that contribute to the promotion of entrepreneurial attitudes, the attainment of entrepreneurial skills, and the improvement of entrepreneurial outcomes. Finally, the findings in this report are intended to inform EET policy and program dialogue at multiple levels, guide investment decisions that policymakers and government institutions make with regard to EET programs, and further research in the EET realm.

Conceptual Framework for EET

Given the diversity of programs and the wide range of economic conditions under which these programs operate, a framework is used that allows a more structured and focused examination as to what kinds of entrepreneurial education and training (EET) programs and what types of outcomes are relevant to these countries. The framework described below was previously introduced in a global study of entrepreneurship education and training programs (Valerio, Parton, and Robb 2014).

Defining EET

A number of international, regional, national, and local actors are taking part in the global experiment of EET. Today, EET is recognized as an established field of study, growing in parallel with the interest of policymakers and students (Mwasalwiba 2010). While a single, generally accepted definition remains elusive, researchers are contributing to an evolving definition (Charney and Libecap 2000; Farstard 2002; Menzies 2003; Isaacs et al. 2007; Dickson, Solomon, and Weaver 2008).Taken together, EET generally reflects both the activity of transmitting specific mind-sets and skills associated with entrepreneurship; as well as education and training programs that seek to engender various entrepreneurship outcomes. As a working definition for this study, *EET represents academic education or formal training interventions that share the broad objective of providing individuals with the entrepreneurial mind-sets and skills to support participation and performance in a range of entrepreneurial activities.*

Types of EET Programs

EET programs can be classified under two related but distinct categories: education programs and training programs. Broadly speaking, both aim to stimulate entrepreneurship, but they are distinguished from one another by their variety of program objectives or outcomes. While differing from program to program, entrepreneurship education (EE) programs tend to focus on building knowledge

Figure 2.1 Classifying Entrepreneurship Education and Training Programs

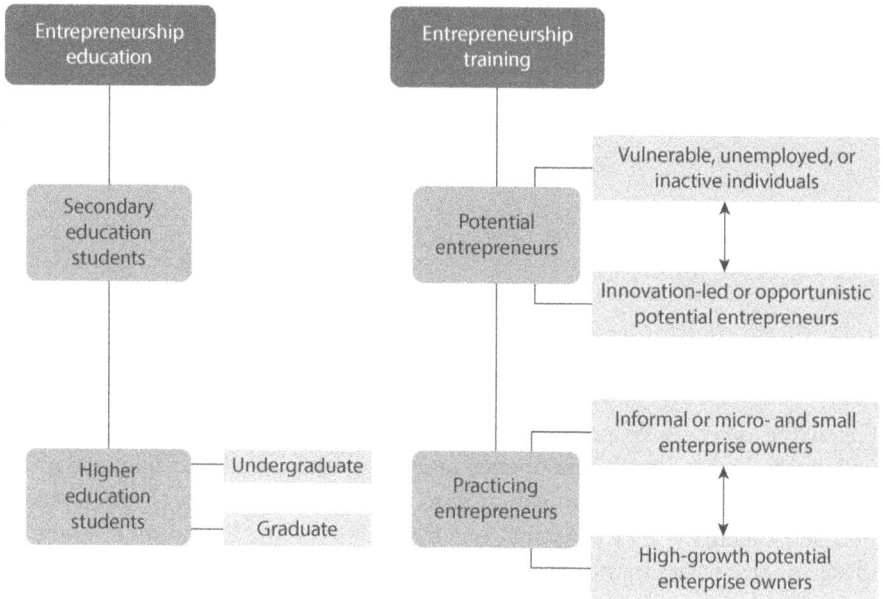

Source: Valerio, Parton, and Robb 2014.

and skills about or for the purpose of entrepreneurship. Entrepreneurship train-ing (ET) programs, by contrast, tend to focus on building knowledge and skills, explicitly in preparation for starting or operating an enterprise.

Advancing the classification of EET, programs can also be distinguished by their target audiences (see figure 2.1). The academic nature of EE means these programs target two groups in particular: secondary education students and higher education students, the latter including both graduate and undergraduate students enrolled in formal degree-granting programs. By contrast, ET programs target a range of potential and practicing entrepreneurs who are not part of for-mal, degree-granting programs. Potential entrepreneurs targeted by ET programs can include, at one end of the range, vulnerable, unemployed, inactive individuals or necessity-driven potential entrepreneurs, and at the other end highly skilled, innovation-led, or opportunistic potential entrepreneurs. Likewise, the range of practicing entrepreneurs runs from individuals owning informal, micro- and small enterprises, all the way to high-growth-potential enterprise owners.

The Dimensions of EET Programs

Determining the outcomes of EET programs is a complex and multidimensional challenge, regardless of whom a program targets. The task is complicated in part because the intended outcomes of EET programs can vary substantially from program to program. Therefore, this study draws upon existing EET research to propose a way of conceptualizing both the results EET programs seek and the factors that can shape those outcomes.

Entrepreneurship Education and Training • http://dx.doi.org/10.1596/978-1-4648-0278-2

Figure 2.2 Conceptual Framework for Education and Training Programs

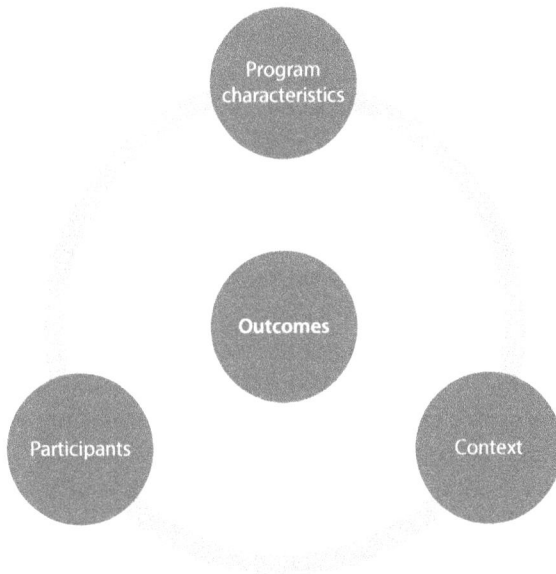

Source: Valerio, Parton, and Robb 2014.

Outcomes for EET programs can be categorized into four domains. The first, *entrepreneurial mind-sets*, refers to the socio-emotional skills and overall aware- ness of entrepreneurship associated with entrepreneurial motivation and future success as an entrepreneur (such as self-confidence, leadership, creativity, risk propensity, motivation, resilience, and self-efficacy). The second, *entrepreneurial capabilities*, refers to entrepreneurs' competencies, knowledge, and technical skills associated with their entrepreneurship (such as management skills, account- ing, marketing, and technical knowledge). The third, *entrepreneurial status*, refers to the temporal state of a program beneficiary as measured through entrepre- neurial activities and beyond (such as by starting a business, becoming employed, or achieving a higher income). Lastly, the fourth domain, *entrepreneurial perfor- mance*, refers explicitly to how indicators of a venture's performance have changed as a result of an intervention (such as by gaining higher profits, increased sales, greater employment of others, or higher survival rates).

The Conceptual Framework also outlines three dimensions that available research has shown to influence the range of EET outcomes (see figure 2.2): (i) the context within which programs are implemented; (ii) the characteristics of individual participants; and (iii) the functional characteristics of the programs themselves.

- *Program context*: The Conceptual Framework accounts for a series of contex- tual influences shown to impact the likelihood of a program's capacity to generate outcomes. These include the economic context, the political con- text, and the cultural context. Studies have looked at the series of economic, political, and social factors that are likely to make individuals more successful at starting new ventures (Pittaway and Cope 2007). As a fundamental example, a market that possesses the unique contextual factors needed to foster entrepreneurship is more likely to have the factors that enable entrepreneurial activity than a market that lacks such contextual factors.

- *Participant characteristics*: The Conceptual Framework also accounts for the moderating influence of what participants bring with them coming into a program. This includes each individual's profile; basic demographic identifiers; personality or traits; education; interest and intentions; and behaviors while enrolled within a program (for example, attrition). These individual characteristics are a prominent subject in the EET literature, and certain personality traits have been linked to positive entrepreneurial outcomes (Luthje and Franke 2003; Rauch and Frese, 2007). From an operational standpoint, EET programs themselves recognize the role of participant characteristics in moderating outcomes. This would explain why so many EET programs use a range of selection processes—screening candidates for various characteristics, including their educational background, their work experience, and even their personalities (using personality tests to screen for certain character traits). Furthermore, program outcomes can be shaped by dynamics associated with participant behavior, including the nature of participant uptake as well as attrition within a particular program.

- *Program characteristics*: The Conceptual Framework distinguishes among four major categories of program characteristics: program design; trainers and delivery; content and curriculum; and wrap-around services. EET programs may range from full academic courses to short training courses. In turn, program characteristics are an important driver of EET, since they are the easiest to manipulate. The entrepreneurship program concept is broader than what can be conveyed by a single course or by the material taught in a classroom alone; instead, it comprises a whole portfolio of complementary activities (Souitaris, Zerbinati, and Al-Laham 2007). An appropriate design of this portfolio is important to a program's ultimate outcomes. The portfolio can include the usual components related to classroom activities—such as trainers, curriculum, delivery format, and duration or intensity—as well as wrap-around services like mentoring, networking opportunities, guest speakers, and collaboration with other institutions.

CHAPTER 3

Context for Entrepreneurship in Ghana, Kenya, and Mozambique

The Conceptual Framework described in the previous chapter highlights how a series of contextual influences shape both opportunities and barriers for entrepreneurs. It organizes these barriers along economic, political, and cultural lines to bring clarity to the range of influences that can shape the environment for potential and practicing entrepreneurs. It is within these environments that entrepreneurial education and training (EET) programs function, and in some cases programs are crafted to respond to them. To better understand the respective contexts that EET programs function within, this chapter provides an overview of the contextual factors that shape the entrepreneurial environment. For each country, the chapter examines key economic, political, and cultural trends. Where appropriate, this also includes information from a series of global entrepreneurship research initiatives that seek to benchmark a country's "friendliness" to entrepreneurs. In addition, this chapter pulls in the perspectives of entrepreneurs from each country based on interviews conducted with them.

Although this chapter describes how in each of the case countries, key macroeconomic trends give reason for optimism about the trajectory of private sector development, entrepreneurs in each of the countries do face considerable barriers. On the one hand, the challenging entrepreneurial environment can be viewed as overwhelming the potential of EET programs to contribute to the success of participants. But on the other hand, it appears that EET programs were intentionally crafted to respond to some of the profound contextual challenges that these countries face, from high youth unemployment to high percentages employed informal sectors. Thus, in looking at these countries' contexts, the diverse landscape of EET programs can be viewed as both weathering and responding to national challenges.

The Economic Context

The "economic context" represents the multiple economic variables that have been found to correlate with entrepreneurship outcomes. In their study of youth employment in Sub-Saharan Africa, Filmer et al. (2014) indicate that two dimensions shape pathways to productive work: the human capital of the individual and the business environment in which the individual operates. In this sense, entrepreneurs' ability to succeed based on their own skills and abilities is moderated by the economic context in which they operate. The World Bank's 2013 development report on jobs states, "Even potentially skilled entrepreneurs would have difficulty succeeding without access to basic infrastructure and financial resources. In their absence, managerial capacity alone may not be enough" (World Bank 2012d). Further, McKenzie and Woodruff (2012) suggest that spillovers (positive or negative) within the economic context from entrepreneurship programs may correlate with entrepreneurship outcomes. Although EET programs often operate primarily within local contexts, national economic trends often shape the local conditions. Following are some of the key national trends discernible in the case-study countries.

Prospects for export-driven growth are significant, and the service sectors are also large

The Sub-Saharan African region experienced profound growth in recent decades, with gross domestic product (GDP) growing more than 4.5 percent a year on average between 2000 and 2012 and with strong prospects for sustained growth over the medium term. Further, in most of the countries in the region growth depends on the export of primary commodities (Filmer et al. 2014). The case countries align with these broader trends. Kenya is the largest economy in east and central Africa and the main hub for the region's financial, communication, and transportation services. Its GDP growth averaged 3.7 percent between 2000 and 2009 (World Bank 2010). Its growth contracted in 2012 (from 4.4 percent in 2011 to 4.3 percent), when its central bank increased interest rates in the fight against rising inflation and the Shilling depreciation (World Bank 2012a). However, Kenya's growth in 2013 was 5 percent, with a strong economic outlook for 2014 (World Bank 2013c). Economic prospects are also positive as a result of the discovery of oil and gas reserves, which are expected to attract high inflows of foreign direct investments and income for the government. Services dominate the economy, accounting for over 50 percent of GDP, with agriculture accounting for 25 percent of GDP and manufacturing (including manufacturing, mining, construction, energy, and water) accounting for around 20 percent. In terms of exports, agricultural commodities dominate; in declining order of volume the country exports tea, horticulture products, apparel and clothing accessories, unroasted coffee, tobacco and tobacco products, iron and steel, and animal and vegetable oils (Government of Kenya 2012).

Ghana, with one of the highest GDPs per capita in Africa, is now one of the top 10 fastest-growing economies in the world and the fastest-growing economy in Africa. Driven in part by a diverse and rich natural resource base and an influx of foreign direct investment, Ghana experienced growth rates in the 4 to 15 percent range for most of the last five years (GSS 2013). Ghana's Statistical Service (GSS) reported a growth rate of 7.9 percent in 2012, down from 15 percent in 2011. However, rather than the fall being indicative of a sluggish or stagnating economic performance, it was due to an inordinately high 2011 figure from commercial oil production. According to the World Bank (2013b, 2), Ghana's growth will be driven by the petroleum sector. As in Kenya, in Ghana agriculture accounts for roughly one-quarter of GDP, while the services sector accounts for about 50 percent of GDP. The services sector has recently recorded the highest growth, at 8.8 percent on average between 2009 and 2013, with five activities in this sector recording growth rates above average: financial interme-diation; information and communication; real estate, professional, administrative, and support service activities; health and social work; and community, social, and personal service activities (GSS 2013).

For the last decade, Mozambique's GDP growth averaged 8 percent between 1993 and 2010 according to the World Bank (2012f). Although it fell in 2009 to 6.3 percent, it has been estimated to have risen to 7.2 percent in 2012. In the manufacturing sector, after a period of remarkable growth, the growth rate has slowed, so that the sector's share of GDP dropped from 16 percent in 2005 to 13.2 percent in 2010. Agriculture accounts for an estimated 31.5 percent of GDP in Mozambique, with growth in the sector driven by the export-oriented subsectors, such as the cotton and sugar industries, and the expansion of land use (NKC Independent Economists 2012). The extractive industries now account for 1.5 percent of total GDP and are poised to increase, in large part due to a series of megaprojects and associated foreign direct investment (AIMO 2010). Meanwhile, domestic small and medium enterprises and locally owned business ventures lag behind and experience low labor productivity.

Modern wage employment is nevertheless scarce.

In Kenya, although wage employment has increased, the Kenya National Bureau of Statistics (KNBS) estimates that only two out of five wage jobs are modern jobs in the formal private sector (2.1 million in 2011). These jobs are spread across sectors, with 800,000 in services, 350,000 in industry, 290,000 in agriculture, and 680,000 in the public sector. Youth, defined in Kenya as between the ages of 15 and 34,[1] constitute two-thirds of the workforce (United Nations Development Programme 2013); and while some 800,000 young Kenyans reach working age each year only 50,000 new modern wage jobs each year are created (World Bank 2012a). In Ghana, it is estimated that two-thirds of the population is employed by the private sector, but less than 20 percent of these workers are employed in the formal sector (Osei-Boateng and Ampratwum 2011). In Mozambique, the formal sector employs 11.1 percent of the total labor force, 4.1 percent of which is in the public sector (Government of Mozambique 2006). These figures are consistent with trends in countries in Sub-Saharan Africa, where it is estimated that about 16 percent of total employment represents for-mal wage jobs (Filmer et al. 2014).

Employment opportunities for young adults are scarce.

The outlook for job opportunities for youth has been getting harder worldwide. According to the International Labour Organization (ILO [2014]), the global unemployment rate for youth rose from 11.6 percent in 2007 to 13.1 percent in

2013. Kenyan census data indicate that unemployment is particularly high among youth; unemployment rates in the year 2009 were highest among those ages 15 to 19 (24.3 percent), 20 to 24 (27.1 percent), and 25 to 29 (25.5 percent).

Moreover, inactivity rates, which measure the share of the population who are neither studying nor working in any form, are substantially higher. For instance, the inactivity rates for the population between ages 15 and 24 in Sub-Saharan Africa have been constant between 2000 and 2010 at around 46 percent (ILO 2013). For youths ages 20 to 24, the inactivity rate was calculated as 11.9 percent, but this rises to 15.6 percent among urban youth.

Similar problems exist in Ghana, where the soaring unemployment rate is considered a serious challenge. It has been reported that as many as 50 percent of graduates who leave Ghanaian universities and polytechnics will not find jobs for two years after their national service, and 20 percent will not find jobs for three years (Aryeetey 2001). The challenge lies not only in tackling the already sizable number of unemployed graduates, but also in absorbing the new entrants into the labor market. One of the biggest weaknesses of the Ghanaian economy therefore is the chronic joblessness of a vast proportion of the people. Similarly, in Mozambique the unemployment rate remains above 21 percent and is higher among young adults, including university graduates; it is estimated that about 300,000 youths enter the labor market there each year (Government of Mozambique 2006). All of this is aligned with the World Bank's report on youth employment in Sub-Saharan Africa, which finds that only around 16 percent of youth find jobs in wage or "formal" positions, whereas the vast majority of jobs are "either on family farms (62 percent) or in household enterprises (22 percent), which may be collectively described as informal sector" (Filmer et al. 2014, 4).

The informal sector accounts for a large percentage of employment.

In Kenya, the majority of new labor market entrants have to rely on work in the informal sector, which is essentially vulnerable employment. As of 2012, around 80 percent of all employment was in the informal sector, and 86 percent of all new jobs created in Kenya were informal-sector jobs (Government of Kenya 2012). As in Kenya, many of the employed in Ghana are self-employed workers who have established enterprises in the absence of formal employment opportunities; these enterprises constitute simple business activities with low entry barriers and low returns, including home-based enterprises, operating mainly in retailing or the production of food and drink (Altenburg 2009). In Mozambique, amid a total labor force of 10.1 million, it is estimated that 52.3 percent are self-employed informal sector workers and that 11.5 percent are family workers without remuneration (Government of Mozambique 2006).

The Political Context

Beyond the fundamental stability of local political institutions, a number of political factors can shape the entrepreneurial environment. Political factors can manifest as specific policy actions that reduce bureaucratic barriers and corruption, ensure fair practices, or provide grants and funding to support entrepreneurial opportunities and promotion programs (Freedom House 2008; Heritage Foundation 2008; World Bank 2012a, 2012b). Governments can also promote entrepreneurship through an explicit entrepreneurship promotion framework or strategy. Moreover, political contexts can be shaped by local actors, including schools and various community-based organizations.

Policies are in place to foster improvements in the business environment and promote private sector development, but considerable barriers for entrepreneurs remain.

Barriers include each country's legal and regulatory frameworks and infrastructure, while issues of corruption and insecurity, particularly in the informal sector, and remain endemic. Interestingly, despite Ghana's comparative political stability and reputation for sound economic management in recent decades, in interviews Ghanaian entrepreneurs expressed deep frustration with the government's support for local entrepreneurship.

In Kenya, the past decade has been characterized by deliberate policies to strengthen the private sector, agreed upon in the Economic Recovery Strategy for Wealth and Employment Creation 2003–07 (ERS) and in Vision 2030, which seeks to transform Kenya into a middle-income country by 2030 (Government of Kenya 2008). The new constitution of 2010 is envisaged to further improve the business climate through devolved policy and decision making, judicial reforms, and empowerment of institutions to fight corruption and red tape. Further, peaceful elections and a smooth transition of government appear to have led to renewed confidence in the economy. Successful Kenyan entrepreneurs indicated that they have witnessed notable improvements in the business climate over the last 10 years, due to the government's efforts focused on improving the legal system, decreasing corruption and red tape, and promoting recognition of the importance of the private sector and its contribution to the country's development. Nonetheless, entrepreneurs indicate that corruption, prohibitively high taxes, and harassment by local government officers remain endemic. Further, crime and insecurity remain a concern, most notably for entrepreneurs with micro- and informal enterprises.

In Ghana, a quarter-century of political stability and relatively sound economic management has contributed to more than two decades of positive economic growth. Over the past decade, Ghanaian policies have aimed at reinforcing stability through support for sustained reductions in poverty levels and the shaping of a competitive business environment. Nonetheless, the Ghanaian economy has yet to achieve the desired structural transformation needed to move the country into the state of a modern, industrialized, and prosperous economy. Moreover, Ghanaian entrepreneurs did not describe a bright outlook for the business climate for entrepreneurs. They felt strongly that the regulatory set-up there was not conducive to the development of local entrepreneurship, with high interest rates, high taxes, and government policies that favor foreign enterprises as opposed to local entrepreneurs. They also felt the government was not doing enough to support entrepreneurs by way of key infrastructure investments, such as roads, water sources, and supply of electricity. Corruption and bureaucratic impediments to registering and licensing a business were also cited as barriers.

In Mozambique, the introduction of the Economic Rehabilitation Program (PRES) in 1987 constituted the first steps towards moving away from a centrally planned economy. In 1990, through a new constitution, the country introduced a multiparty democracy and recognized the role of market forces in efficiently allocating resources. While the Mozambican economy has made significant progress in the last 10 years in its reported growth and its efforts on improving the investment climate, it still has a low ranking in international indicators of competitiveness and business environment. According to World Bank (2012f, 15) the issues are related to poor access to finance, perceived prevalence of corruption, inefficient government bureaucracy, inadequate infrastructure, and the education level of the workforce. Fragmentation in government policy and in the regulatory institutions for economic management contributes to delays and bureaucratic barriers. Further, corruption, crime, and insecurity remain considerable barriers for Mozambique's entrepreneurs in the informal sector (ANEMM 2000; Lopes 2006; AIMO 2010; Marrengula, Nhabinde, and Amosse 2012).

The Cultural Context

Cultural context refers to factors associated with local perceptions of entrepreneurship as well as cultural attitudes toward failure, success, and the traditional roles of certain members of society. These cultural dynamics can either enable or constrain entrepreneurship in a society. Hofstede (1991) defines cultural values as broad tendencies to prefer specific behavioral patterns over others. Specific cultural dimensions (Rauch et al. 2000; Pinillos and Reyes 2011) and the presence of entrepreneurial values within a society (Davidson and Wiklund 1997) have also been associated with different levels of entrepreneurial activity.

Across the case countries, among the most frequently cited barriers to entrepreneurs' success were local attitudes toward entrepreneurship.

Entrepreneurs believe there is a lack of wide acceptance of entrepreneurship as a respected career path. Potential Kenyan entrepreneurs described a pervasive fear of venturing into self-employment as a result of cultural attitudes toward familial financial obligations—whereby it becomes difficult to deny goods or credit to extended family members or relatives—and accompanying discouragement by peers and family members. The lack of family and peer support was also cited by potential and practicing entrepreneurs in Ghana and Mozambique.

Entrepreneurs across the case countries also believe cultural factors can shape the performance of practicing entrepreneurs.

Entrepreneurs in Kenya indicated that certain behavioral patterns (giving out goods for free, diverting business funds to nonbusiness purposes) are cultural and socioeconomic impediments to enterprise growth. In Ghana, entrepreneurs describe how a search for quick money, prejudice, a "pull him down" attitude, and superstition can all compromise many entrepreneurs' willingness to persevere. In Mozambique, entrepreneurs also cite deep-rooted cultural values that thwart entrepreneurial success.

The Entrepreneurial Environment

There are a number of global research initiatives that aim to provide comprehensive measures of countries' business environments, some of which are specifically focused on the conditions for entrepreneurship and the level of entrepreneurial activity. While Ghana, Kenya, and Mozambique are generally low performers across these studies' global samples, there are regional indicators suggesting that these countries are stronger performers among their peers. In turn, many of these regional rankings must be appreciated within the broader context of these countries' level of development. Nonetheless, these research initiatives serve to provide indicators of broad areas and challenges within the business environment with which these countries' entrepreneurs must cope. Overall, while these rankings indicate that life is not easy for entrepreneurs within the case countries, they can inform the extent to which EET programs are meeting the needs of entrepreneurs by helping them address the considerable challenges they face.

Ease of Doing Business

The first among these research initiatives is the World Bank's *Doing Business* project,[2] which assesses regulations affecting domestic firms in 185 economies. It ranks the economies in 10 areas of business regulation, including starting a business, resolving insolvency, and trading across borders. Among the 50 economies that have made the biggest improvements since 2005, the largest share—one third—are in Sub-Saharan Africa. However, the only countries in Africa to make the top 50 are Mauritius and South Africa. Ghana ranks 64th, Kenya 121st, and Mozambique 146th. The same three case countries rank 5th, 10th, and 20th, respectively, among the 46 African countries examined, but there is variation in where the case countries sit among various subfactors.

Ghana, for example, ranks near the bottom (40th out of 46) in dealing with construction permits, but it ranks 2nd in registering property. Kenya ranks 2nd with respect to getting credit, but near the bottom (37th) in registering property. Mozambique ties with Ghana for 5th place in investor protection, but ranks 40th in access to electricity. In terms of starting a business, Mozambique ranks higher than Ghana and Kenya—in 10th place, compared with 14th for Ghana and 23rd for Kenya (See table 3.1).

Global Competitiveness Index

The World Economic Forum's Global Competitiveness Index ranks countries by their competitiveness, as determined by a set of institutions, policies, and other factors that affect countries' levels of productivity.[3] On average, Sub-Saharan African economies trail the rest of the world in competitiveness, with the region being home to 14 of the world's 20 least competitive economies. Among the three countries reviewed in this report, Ghana again ranks first, scoring in 103rd place out of 144 countries. It is followed closely by Kenya (106th), and less closely by Mozambique (138th). The most problematic factors for doing business in Ghana, according to this index, are access to financing, corruption, tax rates, and "poor work ethic in the national labor force." For Kenya, the four most

Table 3.1 "Ease of Doing Business" Rankings in Case-Study Countries

Country	Ease of Doing Business Rank	Filtered Rank	Starting a Business	Dealing with Construction Permits	Getting Electricity	Registering Property	Getting Credit	Protecting Investors	Paying Taxes	Trading Across Borders	Enforcing Contracts	Resolving Insolvency
Ghana	64	5	14	40	3	2	4	5	11	7	5	18
Kenya	121	10	23	3	36	37	2	16	33	25	30	14
Mozambique	146	20	10	29	40	31	22	5	17	16	22	28

Source: World Bank 2013a.

problematic factors are corruption, inflation, tax rates, and crime/theft. The top four problems in Mozambique are access to finance, corruption, inadequate supply of infrastructure, and inefficient government bureaucracy.

Global Entrepreneurship Development Index

The Global Entrepreneurship Development Index (GEDI) ranks 115 countries according to a multidimensional entrepreneurship measure, and incorporates both quality-related and quantitative differences.[4] The index includes both individual and institutional variables, allowing for inter-relatedness between all variables. While Mozambique is not yet included in the rankings, Ghana and Kenya come out near the bottom, ranking 95th and 98th, respectively.

Global Entrepreneurship Monitor

The Global Entrepreneurship Monitor (GEM) project provides an annual assessment of the entrepreneurial activity, aspirations, and attitudes of individuals across a wide range of countries.[5] Unfortunately, only Ghana is included in the current ranking. In comparison with other Sub-Saharan countries, Ghana ranks higher for perceived opportunities and capabilities as well as for entrepreneurial intentions and "high status to successful entrepreneurs," but it ranks lower for "fear of failure." In addition, when the GEM examined entrepreneurial activity, it found that when compared with other countries examined in Sub-Saharan Africa, Ghana has relatively higher rates of new business ownership, early-stage entrepreneurial activity, established business ownership, and improvement-driven opportunity (as a percentage of total entrepreneurial activity). Ghana is on par with the other countries in its rates of nascent entrepreneurship (15 percent) and discontinuation of businesses (16 percent), and it ranks lower in rates of necessity-driven entrepreneurship as a percentage of total entrepreneurial activity.

Monitor Study

A 2012 study by the Monitor Group, funded by the Omidyar Network, examined the state of entrepreneurship in Africa, and included detailed surveys in both Ghana and Kenya, as well as four other Sub-Saharan African countries (Monitor Consulting Group 2012). These countries were then benchmarked against global peers.[6] The survey focused on four aspects of entrepreneurial environments: (i) entrepreneurship assets (financing, skills, talent, infrastructure); (ii) business assistance (government programs, incubation); (iii) policy accelerators (legislation, administrative burdens); and (iv) motivations and mind-sets (legitimacy, attitudes, culture). Figure 3.1 provides a summary from the report, detailing how Sub-Saharan African countries compared with their peers along these four different dimensions.

Interestingly, while Doing Business, Global Competitiveness Index, and the GEDI all rank Ghana slightly above Kenya (and well above Kenya in Doing Business), the country figures from the Monitor Group report suggest that Ghana performs below peers, and below Sub-Saharan Africa more generally, in

Figure 3.1 Entrepreneurial Environment of Sub-Saharan Africa versus Global Peers

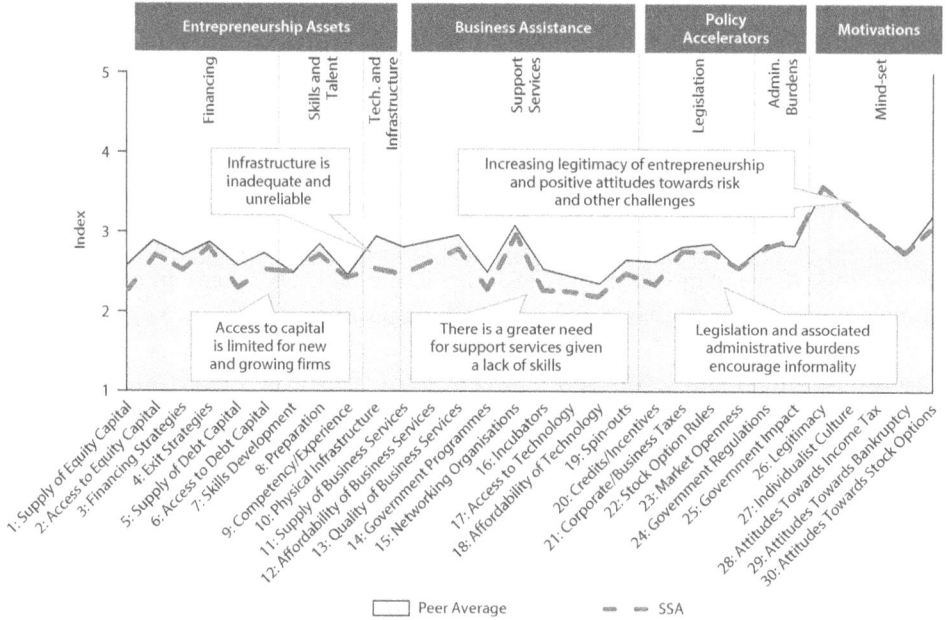

Source: Monitor Consulting Group 2012.

Figure 3.2 Entrepreneurial Environment of Ghana versus Global Peers

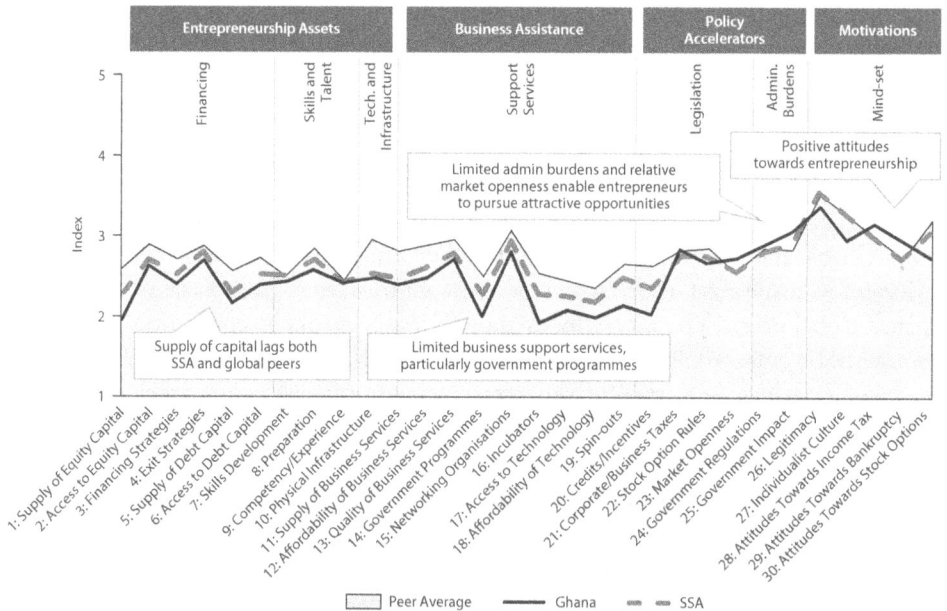

Source: Monitor Consulting Group 2012.

Figure 3.3 Entrepreneurial Environment of Kenya versus Global Peers

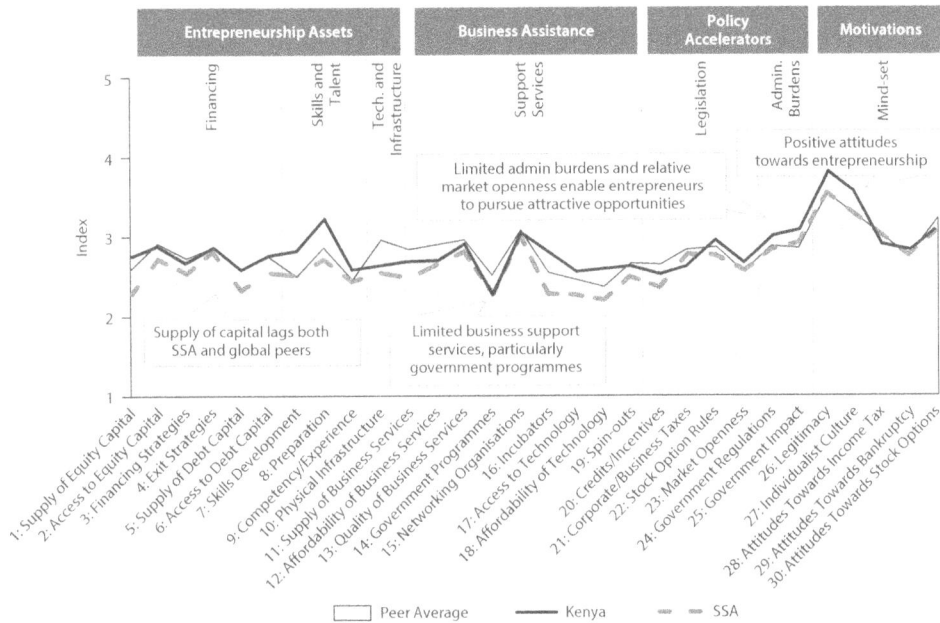

Source: Monitor Consulting Group 2012.

all four of the categories: entrepreneurship assets, business assistance, policy accelerators, and entrepreneurial motivations/mind-set (see figure 3.2). Kenya by contrast, performs well above the Sub-Saharan Africa average according to the Monitor Group in almost all the indicators and generally performs on par or above with all its peers (see figure 3.3).

Current Snapshot

While there is some cause for optimism, the challenges to achieving a vibrant entrepreneurial economy in the region are enormous. And while EET programming can only address a fraction of those challenges, more effective programming has the potential to have a tangible impact in achieving that desired reality.

Potential and practicing entrepreneurs in Ghana, Kenya, and Mozambique have reason for optimism with regard to the expansion of entrepreneurial opportunity.

All three countries are experiencing periods of sustained economic growth, and the diversifying private sector and the less-capital-intensive service sector in particular are increasingly dominant contributors to each country's economy. In comparison to peers in Ghana and Mozambique, Kenyan entrepreneurs are the most optimistic about their economic context. Relative to other countries in Africa, all three countries ranked above average in terms of the ease of doing business there. There seems to be growing recognition of the importance of creating an enabling entrepreneurial ecosystem, especially in Kenya and Ghana.

However, each of the case countries faces considerable structural barriers to eco-nomic transformation, which fosters necessity-driven entrepreneurship and associated barriers to enterprise development.

A relative lack of modern wage jobs and very high structural unemployment, particularly for youth, contribute to the large percentage of individuals employed in each country's informal sector. For many, necessity-driven entrepreneurship in the informal sector is an option of last resort; for those with the potential to grow their enterprises, the lack of formalization fosters insecurity as well as legal and financial impediments to growth. The growing number of unemployed and underemployed college graduates is symptomatic of pervasive barriers to startup activities.

Across the case countries, entrepreneurs cite considerable barriers to entrepreneur-ial success.

Frequently mentioned barriers include corruption, bureaucratic red tape and, above all, lack of access to finance. While these are issues associated with entre-preneurial barriers across the globe, they are featured subjects across the interna-tional rankings featured in this chapter, and they are particularly pronounced in the case countries, given the prevalence of entrepreneurial activity taking place in the informal sector.

Negative cultural perceptions of entrepreneurship persist.

Entrepreneurs in the case countries mention a lack of successful role models and general negative cultural perceptions of entrepreneurship as a challenge. These attitudes may be in part shaped by the visible struggles that local necessi-ty-driven entrepreneurs face, particularly in comparison to those in wage employment, rather than to any endemic cultural distaste for the concept of entrepreneurship. However, the perceived inferiority of entrepreneurship as a career choice will hamper efforts to build a vibrant ecosystem that encourages entrepreneurial endeavors.

EET alone will not be sufficient for addressing the factors that influence entrepre-neurs' fates.

Issues related to access to and the cost of financial capital, as well as integra-tion into markets through market information, regulatory regimes, and infra-structure constraints all have an impact on entrepreneurial outcomes. While such factors are beyond the scope of what any single EET program can address, EET programs would benefit from greater attention to the linkages between improve-ments in knowledge and skills and other enterprise development mechanisms, including access to funding and market intelligence.

There is a notable gap between what the stakeholders' needs and demands are and what the programs deliver.

Among entrepreneurs in the case countries, the desire to complement knowl-edge and skill acquisition with additional supports is understandable. This may be reflected in the growing interest in the region in incubator and accelerator models and other more comprehensive programs that embed EET programming within a broader offering of support services for entrepreneurs, such as office facilities, Internet access, mentors, and financial capital.

Notes

1. The National Youth Council Act of 2009 defines youth as "(…) a person aged between eighteen and thirty-five years" (Government of Kenya 2009, 5).

2. http://www.doingbusiness.org.

3. http://www.weforum.org/reports/global-competitiveness-report-2013-2014.

4. http://cepp.gmu.edu/research/geindex/.

5. http://www.gemconsortium.org.

6. The 6 Sub-Saharan African countries are benchmarked to a peer group, including an additional 13 countries where the Monitor Group has previously undertaken the Entrepreneurship Benchmarking Initiative: Chile, China, Colombia, Denmark, the Arab Republic of Egypt, India, Jordan, the Russian Federation, Singapore, the Republic of Korea, the United Arab Emirates, the United Kingdom, and the United States. This peer group was chosen to allow the focus countries to be compared to a geographically and economically diverse group of countries.

CHAPTER 4

Landscape of Programs

The previous chapter highlighted key trends that have shaped the entrepreneurial environments in Ghana, Kenya, and Mozambique and, in turn, the contexts within which entrepreneurial education and training (EET) programs operate and in some cases are designed to respond to. Against those backdrops, this chapter summarizes the findings from scans of the landscape of EET programs in these three case countries. Using the preceding framework for EET, findings from the countries are organized by program type (entrepreneurship education and training) and target group (secondary and higher education students as well as potential and practicing entrepreneurs). The summaries highlight key program characteristics and, where possible, include information on outcomes that programs aim to achieve. The programs that form the basis of the program landscapes are listed in appendix A (Ghana), appendix B (Kenya), and appendix C (Mozambique).

In addition, for each type of EET program, this chapter reflects on its findings in relation to insights from the global scan of EET program evaluations (Valerio, Parton, and Robb 2014). This comparison makes it possible to understand the extent to which EET programs in the case countries are unique or share similarities with other programs, based on available knowledge about global practice in EET. Further, drawing upon interviews with local potential and practicing entrepreneurs, this chapter offers a discussion of how the landscape of EET programs relates to the specific challenges and opportunities of local entrepreneurs.

Program Landscape Overview

The EET landscape draws upon a comparatively larger and more established set of programs in Kenya as compared to Ghana and Mozambique.

In Kenya and Ghana, 42 EET programs were identified, while 27 programs were identified in Mozambique with sufficient information for the analysis. However, these filtered programs were drawn from a field of a total of 111 identified programs in Kenya, as compared to 80 programs in Ghana and 31 in Mozambique. Further, while a number of long-established programs were identified in Kenya, EET is a comparatively newer phenomenon in both Ghana and Mozambique. In Ghana, nearly half the programs mapped were five years old or younger, and in Mozambique EET programs did not emerge until after the civil war ended in 1992.

Program landscapes suggest that EET is often designed to respond to key contextual challenges.

In Kenya, among the many programs identified, nearly half are classified as entrepreneurship training programs targeting potential entrepreneurs. This reflects the imperative of employment creation in the Kenyan economy, where pervasive and growing youth unemployment is commonly perceived to be a major factor in the country's security problems and political instability. This, coupled with the slow job growth of recent years, has motivated the government to invest in large-scale training programs aimed at supporting youth and the unemployed to venture into self-employment.

In Ghana, which is also facing chronic joblessness among young adults and university graduates, one-third of programs target higher education students alone. Perhaps the most pronounced example of EET catering to a country's context is the situation in Mozambique, where the first generation of EET programs emerged in the early 1990s targeting demobilized soldiers in the wake of the Mozambican civil war. Seen as a potential catalyst to peace and stability through the support self-employment initiatives, the programs were later expanded to target vulnerable groups, in particular women, former refugees, and those severely affected by the war.

Identified training programs frequently rely upon private and international support.

Across the three case countries, private, nongovernmental organizations, and development partners provide substantive support for EET programs. In Kenya, private organizations dominate the EET landscape, both in implementation and in funding, and there is a high level of involvement of development partners in the field of business sector development. While the majority of programs are run and funded by nongovernmental organizations, some are supported by large private firms, both national (such as Safaricom and Chandaria) and international (such as Microsoft, Coca-Cola, and Samsung). In Ghana, a comparatively larger amount of EET programs are run by public entities, yet nearly all receive some donor support or nongovernmental organization funding of some kind. Development partners also became increasingly active in EET in Mozambique in the late 1990s through two key development institutions: the United Nations Development Programme's (UNDPs) Enterprise Mozambique and the United Nations Industrial Development Organization (UNIDO) and All India Manufacturers' Organization (AIMO)'s Industrial Development Advisory Centre (CADI).

Entrepreneurship Education: Secondary Education Students

Entrepreneurship education for secondary education students (EESE) refers to the building of capabilities, skills, and mind-sets about or for the purpose of entrepreneurship and is aimed at expanding the potential pool of future entrepreneurs. In Kenya, EESE is part of the curriculum in all educational streams and levels, including technical and vocational education and training (TIVET), although it is offered as an optional subject. EESE is also integrated in teacher education programs at certificate and diploma levels—especially those programs focused on commerce—and in certificate programs for social and community development. While not compulsory within general secondary education, EESE is offered within the TIVET system as a vocational subject aimed at imparting knowledge about economics and the business sector, designed to be useful to students planning a career in business later on or business studies in higher education.

EESE programs are largely implemented in Kenya following the Know About Business (KAB) approach, a branded methodology developed and internationally disseminated by the International Labour Organization (ILO) to build business awareness among students. KAB is structured as a pre-start-up program, based largely on hands-on, experiential learning (using role-playing games and simulations, for example). While KAB is an international brand, its curriculum is periodically revised (the latest revision known in Kenya is from 2010) and comprises nine modules, including: *What Is an Enterprise?; Who Are Entrepreneurs?; Finding a Good Business Idea;* and *Developing and Operating a Business Plan.*

Similar to Kenya, in Mozambique EESE is also driven by the Ministry of Education. However, it is a more recent development in Mozambique. During the 2000s, in partnership with both the United Nations Industrial Development Organization (UNIDO) and as part of the broader effort *The Program to Reform Technical and Vocational Education and Training* (PIREP), Mozambique launched two major EESE efforts as part of a broader strategy to combat youth unemployment.

- The first effort was a set of curricular reforms aimed at developing life and entrepreneurship skills among students and teachers at the lower and upper secondary levels. In 2007, with financial and technical support from UNIDO, an entrepreneurship curriculum focused on promoting entrepreneurial awareness was implemented across 255 schools, serving around 240,000 students throughout the country and taught by 1,521 teachers. By far, this was and continues to be the largest entrepreneurship education (EE) program in the country.
- A second effort in Mozambique was the infusion of entrepreneurship concepts into the country's technical and vocational education and training system. In 2006, under the PIREP program (with the support of the World Bank and a number of bilateral partners), curriculum reforms combined technical competencies with entrepreneurial skills. Within the broader PIREP curriculum, which aims to integrate education and work for credentials across a number of sectors (agriculture, industrial maintenance, hotel and tourism, administration and management, civil construction, and energy and mining), all students are required to study entrepreneurship modules regardless of their area of study.

Similar to EESE in Kenya and Mozambique, in Ghana EESE targets students across a variety of secondary institutions, including general upper secondary schools, technical schools, and vocational schools. Programs in Ghana are typically delivered using a lecture-based format, with curricula focused on building awareness of entrepreneurship. While most of these programs do not provide wrap-around services, a few programs feature mentorship and networking.

Program Outcomes

A review of EESE programs in the three case countries offered little information by way of program outcomes. Available figures largely pertained to program "inputs" or surveys of student opinions. In Mozambique, available information indicated that between 2009 and 2012, enrollment increased by 41 percent in vocational and technical schools after curricular reforms, which included mandatory entrepreneurship modules. However, the increase cannot be attributed in a rigorous fashion to the inclusion of entrepreneurship in the curricula. In Ghana, EESE programs focus on outcomes related to participants' interest in entrepreneurship, but this is evaluated by seeking student opinions and satisfaction levels with the programs upon completion.

In the absence of outcome reporting, information pertaining to programs' desired outcomes can be inferred by examining the objectives of EESE programs across the countries. A finding of particular interest is that while desired outcomes for EESE programs across the countries are concentrated in the entrepreneurial mind-set domain, notable is the absence of socio-emotional skills. Rather, it appears that EESE programs across the three countries aim to primarily build students' entrepreneurial awareness as well as their broader understanding of business principles and concepts.

In Relation to Global Practice:

- *Little information on outcomes.* The lack of information on outcomes for EESE programs across the case countries echoes the dearth of research on these programs across the region and globally. The lack of rigorous EESE evaluations is partly attributable to the difficulty of measuring these programs' linkages with explicit entrepreneurship outcomes such as enterprise formation or enhanced profits. Further, research acknowledges the practical constraints to interventions influencing secondary education students' becoming self-employed or launching entrepreneurial ventures. One evaluation of an EESE program in South Africa illustrates the challenges (South African Institute for Entrepreneurship, 2006). While the program reports promising results across a number of indicators, including students' entrepreneurial knowledge, skills, and attitudes, the evaluations also found that extraneous factors (socioeconomic profile) were a powerful influence on student performance, in fact more influential than the teaching materials, and that entrepreneurial skill acquisition was not a neat, linear process, but proceeded haphazardly over a prolonged period of time.
- *Use of international curricula.* As described from the program landscape in Kenya, several EESE programs around the globe borrow curricula from an

international brand or franchise—examples include Junior Achievement and the ILO's Know About Business (KAB) program. From a program design standpoint, EESE programs can represent an intriguing blend of the global (international NGOs) and the local (individual schools). The Junior Achievement Namibia program (Mahohoma and Muyambo 2008) reflects the approach in Kenya to using an international curricular brand to scale entrepreneurship across the country.

- *Relying on local teachers for delivery.* A trend across the three case countries was the integration of EESE within the secondary level curricula and delivered during normal school hours. This places the delivery of curricula in the hands of local teachers. Several evaluations of EESE programs recognize the role the teacher can have in shaping a program's outcome and thus pay attention to the need for teachers trained in the specific pedagogies and content of EESE programs (Nakkula and others 2004; Bolstad 2006; Volkmann 2009). In Kenya, where entrepreneurship education has been a compulsory aspect of all levels of TVET since the 1990s, entrepreneurship education has been a part of all teachers' training since 1993 (Farstard 2002). Yet, as discussed more fully next, one desired characteristic of EE teachers is actual entrepreneurship experience, which has often not been the case in these three case-study countries.

Entrepreneurship Education: Higher Education Students

Entrepreneurship education programs in higher education (EEHE) target students enrolled in undergraduate as well as graduate degree-granting programs. Notably, while some these programs claim to prepare students for careers as entrepreneurs, they also aim to prepare them for careers in entrepreneurship promotion as "entrepreneurship facilitators."

In Kenya, universities are increasingly involved in entrepreneurship education. Two public universities, Jomo Kenyatta University of Agriculture and Technology and Kenyatta University, have integrated entrepreneurship concepts in most of their academic programs. Kenyatta University and Mount Kenya University have begun systematically training all faculty in all disciplines in entrepreneurship and management. In addition to infusing entrepreneurship concepts across academic programs, several universities offer full academic programs in entrepreneurship. Within Kenya, Jomo Kenyatta University of Agriculture and Technology is regarded as a pioneer of entrepreneurship education at the higher education level, being the first university in the region to offer a PhD program in entrepreneurship. Notably, universities in Kenya are increasingly linked to entrepreneurship incubator programs, which offer a range of wrap-around services from networking and mentorship connections to access to potential funding sources.

Entrepreneurship education is increasingly prevalent in Mozambique's higher education institutions as well. Examples of EEHE programs are found at three institutions, which combined enroll more than half of the country's higher education students: Instituto Superior de Ciências e Tecnologia de Moçambique

(Institute of Science and Technology of Mozambique), Eduardo Mondlane University, and the Pedagogical University. The first of these hosts the Empresa Junior program, which includes workshops and a business plan competition to provide exposure to entrepreneurship among students. The Pedagogical University, in partnership with UNIDO, designed an entrepreneurship course to train teachers on entrepreneurship development in 2009; entrepreneurship there is both a discipline as well as a cross-cutting focus within the curriculum. At Eduardo Mondlane University students take a required entrepreneurship course regardless of their area of study. This last university has also opened an Entrepreneurship Higher Education School, which runs courses on business management and leadership.

In Ghana, EEHE programs target students across postsecondary institutions, including polytechnics and universities. As in Kenya and Mozambique, here EEHE is offered both as a specialized degree program and as an area of curricular focus across programs and disciplines. Within private institutions, EEHE tends to take the form of specialized programs. As an example, the Entrepreneurship Training Institute in Accra offers both a full degree program as well as a post-graduate diploma in entrepreneurship. By contrast, in public institutions EEHE tends to come in the form of a one-semester core course for undergraduate students. Instructors for EEHE programs have varied backgrounds, ranging from professors and lecturers to consultants and entrepreneurs. Wrap-around services are limited though, and typically involve mentorship.

Program Outcomes

As is true for the landscape of EESE programs, for EEHE programs there is little information in the case countries on the associated outcomes. In Mozambique, schools did not conduct systematic follow-up on student outcomes, and in Ghana, institutional outcomes for programs were limited to enrollment and degree completion. However, looking at the objectives of EEHE programs across the three case countries, it is clear that programs focus on building entre-preneurial capabilities—knowledge and skills associated with entrepreneur-ship—while little attention is given to how many students end up actually launching an enterprise.[1] In Kenya, EEHE students indicated that they viewed the programs as valuable for building their management and business skills in order to be prepared for a career, but there are no systematic follow-ups to verify any positive impact from the programs.

This finding about program objectives is line with what is known about the outcomes of EEHE programs globally. Most evaluations of EEHE programs are largely concerned with measuring the extent to which students were enhancing capabilities associated with entrepreneurial activity and success. This focus is also consistent with the profile of a target group that is still comparatively young, preparing to enter the world of work and, thus, preparing for entrepreneurship. Lending strength to the idea that these programs can *ultimately* contribute to entrepreneurial activity, Martin, McNally, and Kay (2013) find a relationship between entrepreneurship outcomes and academic-focused EET interventions, characteristic of EEHE. They find that that relationship is stronger for the academic-focused EET interventions ($r = 0.238$) than it is for training-focused EET interventions ($r = 0.151$), which are more likely to resemble Entrepreneurship training (ET) program types. Their finding concerns the potential role of EEHE programs in engendering outcomes that are related not only to mind-sets and capabilities but also to entrepreneurial status (such as enterprise start-up) and performance (such as enterprise survivability).[2]

Further, available evaluations of EEHE programs in Sub-Saharan Africa have also demonstrated promising results in building knowledge and skills, though they show mixed results in contributing to future entrepreneurial activity. A rigorous impact evaluation from Uganda provides the most compelling results. The evaluation of the Skills Toward Employment and Productivity program there, which is run at two Ugandan universities (Gielnik and others 2013), indicated that the 12-month curriculum increased the likelihood of treated students starting a business as compared to the control group. The evaluation credited the results to the program's action-based training method,[3] a learning-by-doing approach that provided students with the skills and knowledge needed to start businesses. (In addition, an evaluation of the EEHE program at the Auchi Polytechnic School of Business in Nigeria also found promising results in terms of developing students' managerial skills as well as enhancing their desire to set up small-scale businesses after graduation) (Idogho and Ainabor 2011).

In Relation to Global Practice:

- *A mix of degree programs and cross-cutting approaches to EEHE.* The landscape of EEHE programs in Ghana, Kenya, and Mozambique is a mix of stand-alone degree programs and entrepreneurship modules integrated across disciplines. Kenya shows signs of entrepreneurship education being integrated across programs at universities, while in Ghana entrepreneurship education programs appear to be phenomena concentrated within private universities. In Mozambique, entrepreneurship education has a presence at the country's largest higher education institutions. Looking at evaluations of EEHE programs globally, a key issue of interest is the high level of self-selection these programs involve, with students already interested in entrepreneurships tending to take advantage of the course offerings. The program landscapes in Kenya and Mozambique, however, indicate that in some cases entrepreneurship is a required area of study, particularly for students in business and management programs.

- *Focus on building skills and awareness.* As with EEHE programs globally, EEHE programs in the case countries tend to have ties to general business education and management programs. As such, they are often taught by faculty in these departments and focus on the business side of entrepreneurship, including management, marketing, and accounting. What information is available on the outcomes of EEHE programs suggests that they tend to focus on developing business and management skills. Thus, what differentiates these programs from traditional business and management education is the focus they have on applying these skills in the context of creating new ventures, notably small businesses. To this end, EEHE programs serve to build awareness of entrepreneurship principles, with some programs associating their success with enhancing students' desirability to become entrepreneurs.

- *Use of simulation activities and learning by doing.* A number of the evaluated EEHE programs place emphasis on the knowledge and skills required to develop a business plan as well as contribute to the strategic development of an enterprise. Evaluations from EEHE programs globally indicate that an encouraging tactic for transmitting these capabilities is the use of simulation activities, such as setting up mock enterprises or business plan competitions. Such exercises can represent a learning-by-doing approach, which was supported by the findings of the Skills Toward Employment and Productivity evaluation in Uganda. In the case countries, there were some instances of programs using business plan competitions, for example the Empresa Junior program in Mozambique. However, it is also useful to examine these activities in terms of why young, potential entrepreneurs may find these programs useful. Focus groups of program participants in the case countries indicate that, particularly at the higher education level, programs are too theoretical and there is little exposure to entrepreneurship concepts in practice and entrepreneurs themselves. Global EET research indicates that business plan competitions often feature such exposure through mentorship and coaching opportunities. Further, they may offer exposure to funders and potential sources of finance, the lack of access to which entrepreneurs across the case countries indicate is a key barrier.
- *Thematic ties to high-growth entrepreneurship.* In global EET research the linkages between EEHE and the establishment of high-growth enterprises remains tenuous, yet many EEHE programs appear to deliberately cultivate innovation-driven entrepreneurs and high-growth enterprises. While a similar theme was not apparent across EEHE programs within the case countries, in Kenya it is notable that universities are increasingly involved in developing entrepreneurship incubators, which globally tend to be selective and feature comprehensive wrap-around services to support high-growth entrepreneurs.

Entrepreneurship Training: Potential Entrepreneurs

Entrepreneurship training for potential entrepreneurs (ETPo) programs target a range of participants, who include vulnerable, unemployed, inactive individuals—often necessity-driven potential entrepreneurs—in addition to innovation-led or opportunistic potential entrepreneurs. In Kenya, the majority of ETPo programs are both funded and implemented by private actors, which include local and international NGOs, as well as both domestic firms (Safaricom, Chandaria) and multinational firms (Microsoft, Coca-Cola, Samsung). Around half of identified ETPo programs in Kenya operate on a national scale, including around 10 percent that are associated with international programs, with the remainder being locally or regionally focused. Regardless, most programs have a strong presence in the capital city, Nairobi.

A number of programs in Kenya target specifically marginalized populations, including women, rural populations, and unemployed youth, with the latter group getting significant attention in recent years. A myriad of different programs there aim to address youth unemployment through the promotion of entrepreneurship. These include publicly funded and run programs under the Ministry of Youth Affairs and Sport (MOYAS), the Kenya Youth Enterprise Fund, and the Yes Youth Can program; the last program has funding from USAID, is implemented by Technoserve, and aims to reach half a million young people. While those large-scale programs are national in scope, with branches or locations throughout Kenya, there are other programs with a more localized focus, such as the Kenya Youth Business Trust (KYBT) in Mombasa. There are also instances of ETPo programs targeting youth specifically for careers in the information and communication technology sector. While the last type focus largely on the development of computer and media skills, they do include entrepreneurship training as a component. Examples include the Samsung Real Dreams Program implemented by the African Center for Women, Information and Communications Technology (ACWICT), which targets young women from poor urban neighborhoods and comprises information technology training alongside life-skills and entrepreneurship training.

Other ETPo programs in Kenya target high-growth potential entrepreneurs, though these are comparatively fewer in number. They include business plan competitions that provide training as a component of support, which may also include access to funding, and they tend to be selective with regard to participants, looking to identify committed and potential entrepreneurs with promising business ideas. Examples include the Enablis ILO Safaricom Foundation Business Plan Competition, cosponsored by the ILO, the Safaricom Foundation, Inoorero University, and Chase Bank; and the Jitihada Business PlanCompetition, funded by the World Bank, which in 2012 alone received 3,493 applications from across Kenya. While all applicants to the latter received one day of training, 800 were selected to participate in the full five-day training.

Given the diversity of target audiences for ETPo programs in Kenya, programs exhibit a variety of delivery approaches. Nevertheless, Kenya offers particular insight on large-scale ETPo programs, given the number of programs targeting large populations of unemployed youth. For example, to cope with such large numbers, the Yes Youth Can project uses a peer-peer learning approach. Across a number of youth programs, trainers are recruited from the corps of youth and development officers, professional development workers, and training consultants. Trainers have usually undergone training-of-trainers programs, but typically they have no business experience, while study visits and guest lectures from the business community are rare. There are notable exceptions, such as KYBT Mombasa, where the trainers come from the business community. Interactive training and experiential hands-on training are common across such programs, though not universal.

A notable trend across the three case countries is the number of programs that include wrap-around services or are linked to broader entrepreneurship promotion efforts, such as microfinance lending. For example, in Kenya, MOYAS provides a business awareness session to all those who qualify for loans through

the Kenya Youth Enterprise Fund, which includes periodic sessions with motiva-
tional speakers. Further, linkages are not always specific to entrepreneurship. In
Mozambique, the International Relief and Development (IRD) program's
"Women First" combines entrepreneurship training for rural women who are
potential entrepreneurs with health promotion and human immunodeficiency
virus (HIV)/acquired immune deficiency syndrome (AIDS) prevention.

In contrast to the ETPo landscape in Kenya, which is comparatively domi-
nated by privately driven initiatives, several prominent ETPo programs in
Mozambique are driven by government ministries. These still target a diverse
range of potential entrepreneurs. The ministry-driven nature of ETPo in
Mozambique may be a legacy of EET's role in the country's postwar reconstruction. Administered by the Ministry of Labor, the National Institute for
Employment and Vocational Training was set up in the early 1990s to reintegrate
demobilized fighters and refugees from the civil war. However, as happened in
Kenya, this institute has since turned its attention to offering entrepreneurship
training programs to unemployed youth, in this case through 13 training centers
across Mozambique.

Mozambique's Ministry of Industry and Commerce also promotes entrepreneurship through a number of activities that include the provision of training to
potential entrepreneurs. In 2008, this ministry established the Small and Medium
Enterprise Promotion Institute (IPEME), which runs short courses on starting
new business and managing small and medium enterprises. Further, reflecting a
growing interest in high-growth potential enterprises, the Ministry of Science and
Technology runs a set of incubators and technology parks that aim to encourage
innovation and high-growth potential entrepreneurship. The latter ministry also
coordinates the STIFIMO program,[4] launched in 2012 with support from
Finland, which creates opportunities and supports young Mozambicans with
information and communication technology expertise to create business plans
for start-up enterprises.

In Ghana, a privately funded institute called the Meltwater Entrepreneurial
School of Technology, also known as MEST, selects potential entrepreneurs from
a pool of university graduates to participate in a two-year training program that
includes business, computer programming, software development, product management, finance, marketing, sales, and leadership. After completing the two-year
intensive program, participants pitch a concept for a business and the winning
teams receive seed funding and a place in the coworking space in an incubator
(also with MEST) where they are paired with advisors and mentors, who provide
guidance in their process of building their businesses.

Program Outcomes

Global EET research indicates that the majority of ETPo evaluations tend to
examine the impact of ET on specific, often vulnerable groups of participants,
including women, unemployed youth, and welfare recipients. In targeting these
groups, evaluations pay particular attention to the extent to which these
programs are able to impact their economic well-being. Looking across the landscape of ETPo programs in the case countries, program objectives are also

indicative of a focus on the economic empowerment for marginalized groups. While there is little direct information on the outcomes of identified ETPo programs in the case countries, due in large part to a lack of monitoring and evaluation, available research on ETPo programs in Sub-Saharan Africa provides insight into programs' potential to deliver on objectives.

In McKenzie and Woodruff's (2012) review of ET programs in developing countries, the authors indicate that some of the stronger effects relate to helping potential owners launch new businesses more quickly. This study, however, finds that at least among the more rigorously evaluated ETPo programs, few evaluations look explicitly at rates of new business start-ups. Instead, as appears to have been the approach with the McKenzie and Woodruff review, proxies for business start-up, such as self-employment and increased business income, are more common in these evaluations. In terms of income generation for marginalized groups, rigorously evaluated programs in Sub-Saharan Africa demonstrate promising findings. The Economic Empowerment of Adolescent Girls and Young Women program in Liberia evidenced gains in weekly income and savings among trainees compared to a control group (World Bank 2012e). Furthermore, the WINGS (Women's Income Generating Support) program in Uganda, which targeted poor and capital- and credit-constrained women, also found significant impacts on income, as well as consumption, and savings (Blattman and others 2013). However, there is little evidence to suggest that the training's impacts on new businesses were sustained over time.

Another outcome of interest for ETPo programs in Sub-Saharan Africa is the enhancement of business practices, with several program evaluations indicating improved record keeping, formal registration, access to new loans, and a more strategic orientation of the businesses concerned. For example, the Youth Opportunities program in Uganda (Blattman, Fiala, and Martinez Forthcoming) found improvements in business practices across two-year and four-year intervals. While the promotion of high-growth entrepreneurship is a focus within ETPo across the case countries, there is little available evidence demonstrating ETPos' contributions to the creation of high-revenue or high-employment firms in the long run.

In Relation to Global Practice:

- *A means of poverty alleviation.* The diversity of ETPo programs within and across the case countries echoes the diverse landscape of ETPo programs globally. In the case countries, ETPo programs also tend to target specific groups, often marginalized populations, another shared finding from global EET research. In these contexts, EET is viewed as a means to the end of immediate poverty alleviation, rather than as a means to the end of fostering entrepreneurs and entrepreneurship. Further reinforcing this focus, several ETPo evaluations give attention to participants' psychological and social well-being, such as participants' self-confidence and teamwork. The focus on such indicators is a reminder that many ETPo program evaluations cover interventions aimed at improving the immediate, material well-being of vulnerable populations. Programs that seek to address the health issues and risks facing rural women, such as Women First (in Mozambique), echo this more expansive reach within EET programming.

- *Attention to unemployed youth.* Across the case countries, a common focus is on the use of EET to respond to concerns raised by youth unemployment. Despite the prevalence of this focus, particularly among EET programs in the region, there is little available evidence globally that gives direct attention to the impact of EET on this target group. Aside from programs targeting EEHE students, few evaluations of ETPo have been conducted to support broader knowledge of how well these programs are responding to policymakers' perception of entrepreneurship as a means for combating persistent youth unemployment (Volkmann et al. 2009).

- *Embedded within broader entrepreneurship promotion efforts.* According to available ETPo evaluations, the training components that combine grants with activities such as internships and mentoring services have more impact than simple training programs. Both in the case countries and in the global sample, ETPo programs are frequently embedded within broader support programs that include wrap-around services, such as grants, conditional cash transfers, and follow-up sessions with trainers to provide further technical assistance in implementing new business practices. While this aligns with how these programs often target marginalized populations (providing extra supports), it is a principle that also holds true for programs targeting high-growth potential entrepreneurs. In the case countries, there is a growing interest in incubator/accelerator models that offer such comprehensive support for potential entrepreneurs.

Entrepreneurship Training: Practicing Entrepreneurs

Entrepreneurship training for practicing entrepreneurs (ETPr) comprises programs that target a range of practicing entrepreneurs, including individuals running informal, micro- and small enterprises as well as high-growth potential enterprises. Given the nature of their target group, these programs are primarily concerned with how they can help entrepreneurs survive and succeed, regardless of their type of enterprise.

In Kenya, a number of different service providers offer training for practicing entrepreneurs. These include the Ministry of Trade through the Kenya Institute of Business Training (KIBT), a comparatively established provider, as well as various business membership organizations (such as the Kenya Association of Women Business Owners (KAWBO) and the Young Entrepreneurs Association). The participation of associations in ETPr programs is a notable distinction within the program landscape in Kenya as compared to the other case countries. It should be noted, however, that in several cases such programs are cofunded by development partners.

The landscape of programs in Kenya indicates that ETPr programs tend to be short, often lasting only one day, to cater to the time limitations that practicing entrepreneurs face. Because training is short, it often focuses on specific topics related to business management, such as human resource strategies and export regulations, and it provides only limited wrap-around services. There are also examples of longer programs, some of which support longer-term goals such as market integration (such as the Entrepreneurship and Handicraft for Exports program and the Supplier Diversifying Program implemented by KAWBO), as well as micro- and informal enterprises. For example, the Street MBA program requires 80 hours of training, covering management, marketing, accounting, business ethics and business English modules, plus an additional 60 hours of computer training.

Furthermore, ETPr programs in Kenya are often tailored to supporting certain groups of entrepreneurs. This includes programs that provide training for micro-finance clients, programs focused on supporting entrepreneurs in specific sectors such as agriculture and information and communication technology, and pro-grams supporting proximate groups of entrepreneurs, such as those running informal enterprises, a category known in Kenya as *jua kali* enterprises. As an example of the latter, the Micro and Small Enterprise Training and Technology Project (MSETTP) provided training to *jua kali* entrepreneurs, people who in many cases are master craft workers in traditional craft occupations (such as metalwork and woodwork), running established enterprises that are often orga-nized in clusters and business associations. MSETTP provided training to 35,000 such proprietors between 1994 and 2002, to support the development of the *jua kali* sector through a training voucher program that subsidized skills and management training.

In Ghana, there are additional examples of a similar focus in ETPr programs on supporting clusters of entrepreneurs, with attention to entrepreneurs in the informal sector, as in Kenya. One program, run by the Ghana National Association of Garages, provided training to 1,000 metalwork craft workers operating micro-enterprises in the Suame Magazine, an area located in the city of Kumasi. Another program aimed at supporting better business practices to improve record keeping and boost sales as well as profits. An additional program in Ghana, operated by the Millennium Development Authority, provided training through farm-based organizations and loose associations of farmers across the country; it was organized to enhance business practice as a means of supporting better crop yields and improving farmers' access to finance.

The landscape of ETPr programs in Mozambique reflects a focus on support-ing the success and growth of enterprises through market integration. Through the Institute for Export Promotion (IPEX), the Ministry of Industry and Commerce runs a program for enterprises with export potential. The program, based in Nampula, serves members of the local association of handicraft produc-ers, offering training in business management, quality control, marketing, and establishing linkages between buyers and sellers. Three other programs explicitly target growth-potential entrepreneurs: the U.S. Agency for International Development (USAID)-Technoserve and Holland SNV programs provide management training, mentorship, counseling, and access to finance in order to support value-chain integration of entrepreneurs producing cashews, peanuts, pepper, and honey. The PACDE program, run by Mozambique's Ministry of Industry and Commerce, offers competitive funding for entrepreneurs looking to invest in their business and their managerial skills. Started in 2011, PACDE organizes training from private service providers and covers 50 percent of the cost, with the business covering the rest. Most participating entrepreneurs run small to medium-sized enterprises.

Program Outcomes

While the available information on the outcomes of ETPr programs identified in Ghana, Kenya, and Mozambique is limited, it is comparatively rich compared to other types of EET programs. Apparent from the program landscape is the focus on enhancing participants' entrepreneurial capabilities, often in the form of improving business practices. The evaluation of the Ghana National Association of Garages program (Mano et al. 2011) found that training fostered the adoption of recommend practices, such as improved record keeping, in comparison to a control group. The evaluation further indicated that the use of better business practices improved enterprise performance outcomes for trainees, including growth in profits and survivability. Similar findings emerged from the evaluation of the MSETTP program in Kenya targeting *jua kali* entrepreneurs (World Bank 2005), which indicated that compared to a control group, the training contributed to improved profits and sales for, and investment in, a significant proportion of trainees. Two rigorous evaluations of programs in Sub-Saharan Africa also reflect these findings. These programs include Promotion of Rural Initiative and Development Enterprises Limited in Tanzania (Bjorvatn and Tungodden 2010), a program targeting small-scale microcredit entrepreneurs, whose evaluation found gains in business knowledge as measured by multiple-choice tests given to participants; and the Women's Entrepreneurship Program (WEP) program in South Africa (Botha, Nieman, and van Vuuren 2006), which demonstrated statistically significant gains across several skill areas, including business knowledge and business skills.

While these results are promising, global EET research is unable to draw a conclusive line connecting enhanced knowledge, skills and practices, and the subsequent performance of an enterprise. A systematic review of evaluations of business training programs by McKenzie and Woodruff (2012) indicates that while EET can have modest effects on entrepreneurs' decision to implement better business practices, few EET studies find significant impacts on profits, sales, or enterprise survivability. A meta-analysis by Cho and Honorati (2013) produces similar findings, demonstrating that improved business practices within an enterprise do not necessarily coincide with improved business performance. A particular issue cited within the available evaluations of ETPr programs in the case countries is the extent to which improved business practices, transmitted through training programs, are sustained once the training programs are complete. Perhaps tellingly, participants in the Growth Oriented Entrepreneurs program in Kenya indicated that while they considered the training valuable, there was a common sense that the program would benefit with more follow-up (ILO 2010).

In Relation to Global Practice:

- *The role of business associations.* A notable trend across all three of the case countries is the involvement of business associations in the provision of training for practicing entrepreneurs. This trend is less pronounced within the global landscape of EET programs, but it may be particularly relevant to the context of the case countries. In some cases, the role of business associations appears to facilitate more training that is short-term or just-in-time, valuable to busy practicing entrepreneurs, while still offering a degree of continuity as well as built-in opportunities for mentoring and networking, characteristics supported by global EET evidence as well as valued by entrepreneurs. Further, by nature of being associated with these associations, such programs tend to have a sectoral focus as well as a broad interest in sectoral development, including facilitating opportunities for integrating entrepreneurs into value chains and markets.
- *The market for training programs.* Across the case countries, there are also instances showing how ETPr programs relate to a market of training programs for practicing entrepreneurs. The market for EET is a relatively unexplored aspect of global EET research, yet examples of how these markets are cultivated and function emerge from the case studies. The MSETTP program in Kenya, which provided vouchers for *jua kali* entrepreneurs to put toward training programs, mentioned specifically in the evaluation how the vouchers spurred growth in the training market. Further, the experience of the PACDE program in Mozambique, which provides competitive funding for training expenses, also mentions the availability of a market of fee-based training for recipients to choose from. The concept of a market for ETPr programs introduces a number of potential dynamics, including how participant behavior and outcomes function given the self-selection factors as well as the idea of participants having "skin in the game." What remains less clear, though, is the extent to which these markets may exist only as responses to available funding from intermediaries (such as through vouchers or competitive grants) as well as how responsive programs offerings may be to the demands of participants.

Linkages with finance institutions. Insights from global EET research suggest that participants in ETPr programs experience improved access to loans. However, this may say more about the sponsors of this type of training—commercial banks and microfinance institutions, for example—than it says about the quality and content of the training itself. The findings from the program landscape echo this trend, with training often made compulsory by microfinance institutions to improve the financial and credit management skills of borrowers as a means of increasing their chances of success. In the case countries, one sees instances of this within microfinance group lending schemes, such as the Faulu Microfinance Bank Limited and Yehu programs in Kenya. Within these programs, credit officers provide the training as part of the routine coaching of credit groups and use outcome indicators that are intertwined with loan outcomes, such as repayment rates and business survival.

Notes

1. Most program staff indicated there was no funding for tracer studies that would allow them to follow participants after they had left the programs.

2. They note that, "Academic-focused EET, with its broader conceptual and theoretical content may be more likely to allow students to make decisions in the highly ambiguous and dynamic contexts that are required to achieve financial success and maintain a business over an extended period of time" (Martin, McNally, and Kay 2013).

3. An action-oriented entrepreneurship training is based on the propositions of action regulation theory (Frese and Zapf 1994). Such trainings feature the following components: teaching the training content in the form of action principles, learning-by-doing, providing positive as well as negative action feedback, and matching training tasks and real-world tasks to increase transfer. The training thus goes beyond other trainings, which focus mainly on learning-by-doing.

4. STIFIMO stands for Programme of Cooperation in Science, Technology and Innovation between Finland and Mozambique 2010–14.

CHAPTER 5

Findings from the Field

A key question that each case study sought to inform is how to design entrepreneurial education and training (EET) programs so they effectively address the relevant barriers to entrepreneurship in a given country. To address this, a series of interviews and focus groups was conducted in each case-study country with five target groups: program managers, successful entrepreneurs, failed entrepreneurs, potential entrepreneurs in EET programming, and practicing entrepreneurs in entrepreneurship training (ET) programming. A standard question methodology was used for each of the three countries to gather information about interviewees' general perception of the entrepreneurial ecosystem, success factors for and barriers to entrepreneurship, and what works and what does not work in EET programming.

Overview of Qualitative Fieldwork

A number of insights of interest emerge from the qualitative fieldwork, only a portion of which are highlighted in this report. It should be noted first, however, that overall most respondents appreciated the value of EET, while there are some specific areas where countries differ in their general perceptions. For example, respondents in Kenya saw EET as useful in preparing people for a business career. This perception is more pronounced in relation to actual business skills and technical competencies, but is less clear in relation to business attitudes and mind-sets. In Ghana, most participants felt that EET programs were successful in providing critical general business skills (management, marketing, sales, human resources) and financial skills (accounting, budgeting, capital structure), but less so in terms of thinking and problem solving skills and soft skills (communication, leadership, presentation, negotiation). A common perception in Mozambique was that some courses were too basic or repetitive or did not take into account the experience and knowledge of participants in selecting and grouping them.

Furthermore, as the framework for this paper acknowledges, EET programs are heterogeneous. Therefore, it must be noted that in the qualitative fieldwork,

there were in some cases discernable differences in the perceived value of program dimensions that more closely related to either entrepreneurship education
(EE) or entrepreneurship training (ET). For example, the value that respondents
placed on supporting the development of socio-emotional skills early on is an
insight generally more relevant to EE programs than to ET. On the other hand,
respondents' belief in the value of specific wrap-around services to address business environment constraints, such as access to finance, is generally more relevant
to an ET audience than to secondary education students. These distinctions cannot not be ignored, but neither should they obscure the commonalties or how
the qualitative fieldwork contributed to a multistakeholder and comprehensive
perspective of what is valued within EET in the region. The qualitative fieldwork
found that while distinctions exist depending on respondents' experience and
respective target group, EET programs operate in the case countries as a diverse
landscape, one that is by no means as ordered or as linear as any framework
would suggest. This presented a unique opportunity to capture several cross-
cutting ideas about the value of EET programs with applicability across a range
of program types.

Thus, with these varying viewpoints in mind across countries as well as types
of EET programming, this chapter profiles the key areas of commonality that
emerged, which form useful insights for informing EET program design. The
chapter first summarizes some of these cross-cutting themes across the case
countries based on what respondents found to be valuable in EET programs and
what needs improvement. Where relevant, the chapter also introduces findings
from global EET research (as captured in Component One of this study) to
support the insights of interviewees and focus group participants.[1] Lastly, this
chapter offers a set of promising practices in EET that have emerged from both
the field work and existing research covering EET programs in Sub-Saharan
Africa. Taken together, this information seeks to provide guidance as to how EET
programs in the case countries can be brought closer in line with the needs of
participants (as articulated by respondents) and emergent promising practices
emanating from EET research.

Building Entrepreneurial Mind-Sets

Unanimously, respondents mentioned business acumen and personal attitudes as
the most important factors in determining success and failure in business, including commitment, passion, humility, perseverance, integrity, hardworking, discipline, patience and resilience, loyalty toward the business, belief in success, and
vision. Important in this context, and mentioned in particular by successful
entrepreneurs, were traits related to long-term commitment (such as patience,
vision, and perseverance) that would help entrepreneurs to overcome unavoid-
able problems and economic slumps.

Respondents in Kenya placed a particular emphasis on the socio-emotional
skills of entrepreneurs that enable them to navigate these challenging environments. In Ghana, six successful entrepreneurs also emphasized the importance of

these mind-sets in their success. Only in Mozambique was the role of mind-sets in entrepreneurial success comparatively downplayed. There, potential and established entrepreneurs alike mentioned that management skills were of paramount importance if their businesses were to be successful. The young and potential entrepreneurs with technical backgrounds connected these skills with the ability to develop business plans and access finance. Nonetheless, they still felt that most EET programs focused more on general business and financial skills and less on socio-emotional skills such as critical thinking and problem solving.

These sets of socio-emotional skills are one key component of the entrepreneurial mind-sets that EET programs globally aim to promote. Yet, generally, respondents who were classified as successful entrepreneurs tended to share a comparatively less positive perception of the effectiveness of existing EET programs, particularly in Kenya and Ghana. Notably, however, their critique seemed less grounded in the potential of EET programs than in the significant challenge posed by the negative entrepreneurial mind-sets perceived to be endemic to their local communities. They felt that these negative mind-sets were so ingrained that it was unlikely that EET programs, particularly short-term programs, would be able to combat them. Respondents across countries and respondent groups did believe in the importance of exposure to entrepreneurial thinking and behavior at a very young age. Most of the successful entrepreneurs who were interviewed highlighted how important the experiences of entrepreneurial parents were for their own development and determination. In Kenya, it is commonly perceived that this exposure tends to differ between the major ethnic groups.

However, respondents who participated in EET programs indicated that EET programs are falling short of meeting this need. In Kenya, most respondents appreciated the value of EET in preparing people for a business career, but less in so in relation to building attitudes and mind-sets. In Ghana, respondents felt that EET programs were successful in providing critical general business skills (management, marketing, sales, human resources) and financial skills (accounting, budgeting, capital structure) but less so in terms of thinking and problem solving skills, and other socio-emotional skills (communication, leadership, presentation, negotiation). In Mozambique, EET participants also believed there was a critical gap in building socio-emotional skills such as communication, leadership, and negotiation, as well as in critical thinking, decision-making, problem-solving, and creative thinking skills.

Despite calls for a focus on building entrepreneurial mind-sets, particularly on developing socio-emotional skills, within the landscape of programs in the case countries one finds few examples of this in local EET programs. This contrasts with trends observed in entrepreneurship education for secondary education students (EESE) research, which reflect an interest in promoting the foundational skills and knowledge associated with entrepreneurship. Programs in the case countries did tend to focus on building entrepreneurial awareness early on, a fact that is consistent with findings from EESE programs globally. However, there is little mention in programs of building skills such as self-efficacy, need for achievement, risk-taking, social orientation, persistence, creativity, and locus of control. Evaluations of EESE programs provide some preliminary support for the role of secondary schools as a means for ensuring that young people possess knowledge, capabilities, and attitudes associated with entrepreneurship (Isaacs et al. 2007); as such, education could serve as the foundation for a more focused entrepreneurial training at a later point in time (ILO 2011).

The idea that EET should provide early exposure to entrepreneurship finds support in broader entrepreneurship research that examines how early exposure in their parents' businesses influences both the likelihood of pursuing entrepreneurship as a career and the subsequent performance of the children's entrepreneurial ventures (Fairlie and Robb 2007). In this sense, EET, particularly programs targeting secondary education students or younger, can play a role in exposing a broader swath of young people to both the option and the desirability of the option to pursue entrepreneurship at a later time. Among the case countries as well as globally, Kenya provides an example of a country that has aimed to institutionalize EET by mainstreaming it into the public education system. In turn, Kenya offers a promising example of how exposure to entrepreneurship can be scaled. But it should be noted that there is less robust support for how the Kenya experience relates to the other desired element of entrepreneurship mindsets: developing relevant socio-emotional skills.

In Kenya, entrepreneurship is part of the formal curriculum in all educational streams and levels apart from formal primary education, including technical and vocational education and training (TIVET) and nonformal education. In the formal TIVET system, EET is compulsory and examinable. Most EE programs in Kenya are implemented following the Know About Business (KAB) approach, a branded methodology for entrepreneurship education aimed at creating business awareness among students, which was developed and internationally disseminated by the International Labour Organization (ILO). It clearly targets potential business start-ups and could also be labeled a "pre-start-up" program. KAB can be considered a teaching methodology that is hands-on and experimental and concentrates on practice learning (including role games and simulations).

Kenya was one of the first countries where KAB was tested on a large scale. The program is currently very widespread in postsecondary TIVET institutions under the Ministry of Higher Education, Science and Technology (though not yet in Youth Polytechnics under MOYAS), as well as in secondary schools and higher education institutions. KAB is used in regular EE classes, but also in extracurricular activities, such as Entrepreneurship Clubs. The latter are frequent in TIVET institutions. The KAB methodology has been introduced in many of the teacher training schemes in Kenya. According to the regional KAB coordinator, most instructors in TIVET institutions have been trained in the methodology, and KAB is integrated in the curricula of the technical training institutes. The curricula are supposed to be regularly reviewed and revised, but the government often lacks the funds to conduct the revisions. As of this writing, a considerable revision is due based on the recommendations of the Task Force on Education from January 2012.

In spite of the scale, at this point there is little systematic knowledge about the effectiveness of the programs in terms of increasing entrepreneurial mind-sets. Since tracer studies are not systematically conducted in the educational or TIVET system, there is no follow-up and no monitoring of KAB, or indeed of EE in general, in Kenyan schools, apart from assessments of learning achievements as part of the general school exams, and quality assurance activities of the Ministry of Education. There is no formal network of KAB teachers or any other structure that would accommodate systematic evaluation of implementation and implementation results and process learning.

Affording Exposure to the Business Community

A common theme emerging from the interviews and focus groups was an expressed desire for more exposure to the business community within EET programs. EET program participants suggested that EET was most valuable when led by instructors with business and entrepreneurial experience. In Kenya, this issue was prominent within discussions about entrepreneurship education programs delivered within postsecondary schools, particularly in the TIVET system. In Mozambique, focus groups and interviews suggested a lack of well-qualified teachers, even though teachers had been specially trained to deliver programs at secondary and vocational/technical schools (but were not experienced entrepreneurs themselves).

Respondents suggested that while to some extent an instructor can offset a lack of business experience with pedagogical skills, an instructor with business experience would be more valuable, since content tends to be too theoretical and academic in nature. Lending support to the idea of more exposure to the business community within EET, global research supplies examples of programs with promising results using a blend of instruction by teachers and local members of the business community. For example, the BizWorld program in the Netherlands (Huber, Sloof, and van Praag 2012) includes a local business person as a volunteer instructor, while in the NFTE program in the United States (Nakkula et al. 2004) local business people serve as volunteer mentors for students to complement a curricula led by a teacher.

Further, respondents indicated that mentorship and coaching is a valued wrap-around service that could also afford exposure to the business community. Across the case countries, interviewees and focus groups shared the importance of systematic mentorship arrangements to offer support and advice as well as stories from real-world experience that help internalize the entrepreneurial mind-sets and concepts. Groups of potential and practicing entrepreneurs emphasized that supportive arrangements should be sufficiently long (and structured) to coach a participant through a start-up phase. There are examples of programs within EET research that echo this emphasis on mentorship and coaching as a wrap-around service. This is evident particularly within the INJAZ (Junior Achievement for Youth in Middle East) program, which targets upper secondary education students across the Middle East (Reimers, Dyer, and Ortega 2012), as well as the Endeavor program, which targets high-growth-potential entrepreneurs in South Africa (IFC Monitor 2006) and the Meltwater Entrepreneurial School of Technology (MEST) program in Ghana, which supports postgraduate students though two years of additional education and then another 18 months of training and support through the start-up phase.

There were few identifiable examples of programs within the case countries that offered the exposure to the business community that local EET participants as well as failed and successful entrepreneurs indicated they desired. In their view, this was an essential component of an effective program, but current examples were few and far between. Interestingly, this appears to be something valued not only within programs targeting secondary educations students but all the way up to practicing entrepreneurs. However, whether the benefit comes in the form of role-modeling to combat negative perceptions of entrepreneurship, or timely and personalized business advice, focus groups acknowledged the challenge of organizing and sustaining such services and opportunities. From a program design standpoint, using instructors from the business community or creating mentorship opportunities may be difficult, impractical or expensive to organize, particularly on a large scale.

If the value of exposure is in part grounded in creating a network to support potential and practicing entrepreneurs, an example from Kenya offers an interesting example of how this networking can be brought to scale. The Kuza Biashara program uses incentives that create value for established entrepreneurs to enter into a network that potential entrepreneurs can benefit from. A large-scale program to empower existing business owners, Kuza Biashara offers ET alongside a large number of services, including website production, general business consulting (phone hotline), mentorship, and networking. With a membership of 50,000 across the country, an important focus of the program lies in mentorship between established members and emerging entrepreneurs, including in-person events with members of the business community. To support bringing this network together, subscribing members of the Kuza Biashara program are offered a subsidized mobile phone subscription by Safaricom, the leading mobile phone company in Kenya.

Tailored and Practice-Oriented Programs

Related to the respondents' sentiments regarding the need for more exposure to the business community within EET programs, there was a desire for more tailored and practice-oriented approaches to EET across the case countries. Concerning programs being more tailored, in all three countries it was noted that participants come into EET programs with different goals and aspirations. Thus, one valued factor is designing programs to meet the specific needs of targeted participants. Many felt that the programs didn't adequately assess the needs of the potential participants of the program and then tailor the curriculum of the program appropriately.

For example, a common perception in Mozambique was that some courses were too basic or repetitive or did not take into account the experience and knowledge of participants in selecting and grouping them. Another important issue, mentioned in relation to programs aiming to support unemployed youth, was the challenge of targeting this heterogeneous group, for example the difficulties that arise when combining trainees with significantly different educational backgrounds or of different ages. A better targeting of programs, as well as more homogeneous group composition, was generally perceived to be important to ensure productive learning. A proper needs assessment of participants was emphasized, particularly in training programs, where the selection of participants should be made based on their level of experience, their knowledge and skills, or the business sector they belong to, so that plenary and group discussions would be productive and interesting to all. It was emphasized that focusing on a particular business sector of potential or practicing entrepreneurs can render EET more homogenous. In Kenya, there appears to be a particular focus on supporting entrepreneurs in specific sectors, such as agriculture and information technology.

Respondents across the case countries also favored EET that is practice oriented. This includes experiential learning methods such as simulations, mock businesses, role playing games, and business plan competitions, as well as field trips to enterprises to see business practices first-hand in real-life conditions. EET research tends to support such approaches, which use "learning by doing" methods (ILO 2011). One particularly promising example of this is the Student Training for Promoting Entrepreneurship program in Uganda, which employed a rigorously tested "action-oriented" approach (Gielnick et al. forthcoming). The program targeted nonbusiness undergraduate students at two Ugandan universities and was taught on a weekly basis over 12 weeks. Student Training for Promoting Entrepreneurship emphasized a range of socio-emotional skills such as leadership, the psychology of planning, personal initiative, persuasion, and negotiation. Perhaps the most distinguishing feature of the program was the use of action-oriented courses, in which training content focused on action principles and learning-by-doing, providing positive as well as negative action feedback, and matching training tasks and real-world experiences.

The Student Training for Promoting Entrepreneurship evaluation investigated how action-based entrepreneurship training transmitted its effects on entrepreneurial action and creating a start-up. As a randomized controlled field experiment, Student Training for Promoting Entrepreneurship evaluated the effectiveness of an action based entrepreneurship training program on entrepreneurial self-efficacy, action knowledge, action planning, entrepreneurial goals, entrepreneurial action, business opportunity identification, and business ownership. Among the findings, the evaluation found that action knowledge was a central factor promoting the initiation and maintenance of entrepreneurial activity. Compared to the control group, the training increased the likelihood of starting a business by 50 percent, and compared to the initial status in the training group the training increased the likelihood of starting a business by 219 percent. The training also had a positive and significant effect on entrepreneurial self-efficacy, action knowledge, action planning, and business opportunity identification.

With regard to content, respondents supported a focus on the use of practical examples of entrepreneurs' experience, and they emphasized the core importance of business and management practices. Solid "hard-core business skills" (as one young potential entrepreneur put it) are considered indispensable for success in business, and there was an emergent consensus that training in business management is a *must* in any entrepreneurship ET program. The call for more emphasis on this front may offer the most promise for EET to fill the needs of potential and practicing entrepreneurs, with several evaluations indicating that EET can support the acquisition and implementation of better business practices in the region and beyond.

From a program design standpoint, the call for more tailored and practice-oriented EET in the case countries presents some challenges as well as opportunities. Notably, some respondents appeared to tie the concept of tailored training to class size. Participants within the public MOYAS-organized ET courses in Kenya, which usually operates with group sizes of up to several hundred, claimed that the sheer size of the classes prevented the course from meeting the needs of participants, including learner-centered presentations, interactive learning, discussions, and even the asking of questions. This raises concern for any large-scale EET intervention targeting large and heterogeneous populations such as unemployed youth.

Overall, these desires for EET programs appear to stem from the broader critique that EET tends to be too theoretical in the eyes of respondents in the case countries. One innovation from Kenya, however, may offer an example of a promising mix of the desired tailored and practical training. Traditional apprenticeship training in Kenya's informal *jua kali* sector is a common pre-employment training scheme targeting youth from poor households, mainly those with low educational attainment. It is primarily a technical skills training scheme, but being attached for months or years (depending on the contract between the master and apprentice) the trainee would usually be exposed to the real business environment and eventually learn sufficient entrepreneurial and business skills to become a self-employed craftsperson. Building on this apprenticeship model, the Private Sector Internship and Training Program under the World Bank-funded Kenya Youth Empowerment Program (KYEP) organizes three-month internships of unemployed youths in selected *jua kali* enterprises. The scheme involves financial support for both the master craftsperson and the apprentice. To make the master craftspersons "better employers," the program has facilitated initial ET for the participating *jua kali* operators comprising entrepreneurship, production, marketing, human resource development, and couching/training practice. This complementary ET for the trainers is provided in the evening hours and is free for master craftspersons.

Comprehensive Approaches to Address Business Environment Constraints

As described in chapter 3, entrepreneurs in each of the case countries face considerable constraints to success from the business environment. Reflecting this reality, respondents indicated that EET alone is typically not sufficient for addressing the many factors that influence entrepreneurs' fates. Prevalent among these constraints across the case countries are issues related to access to—and the high cost of—financing, as well as integration into markets through market information, regulatory regimes, and infrastructure constraints. While acknowledging that such factors are beyond the scope of what any single EET program can address, respondents indicated that EET programs would benefit from greater attention to the linkages between improvements in knowledge and skills and other enterprise development mechanisms, including access to funding and market intelligence. As part of a more comprehensive and long-term approach to EET, programs can focus on equipping participants with skills and knowledge to navigate specific constraints as well as include complementary wrap-around services.

Across the case countries, respondents believed the provision of wrap-around services by EET programs to be the exception rather than the rule. For example, in Mozambique, only a handful of identified programs (Manica High Polytechnic School, Mozlink linkages program, USAID-Technoserve, SNV, IPEX) have comprehensive wrap-around and advisory services to support potential or existing entrepreneurs. The lack of these wrap-around services was a source of dissatisfaction for the majority of those interviewed. In Kenya, comparatively more programs were wrapped with some complementary services, and these were generally seen as essential to program success. In view of the significance of the capital needs of young entrepreneurs, credit provision or at least facilitation of access to finance were among the most valued wrap-around services. When attendance in an EET program was a compulsory precondition for access to credit (for example, in the case of KYBT Mombasa), this was often the driving force for youth to participate. Business plan competitions, connected with cash prizes for the best business ideas, were considered an ideal mechanism to link access to finance with innovative efforts, creating an incentive for EET program participants to perform.

While wrap-around services were perceived to be generally valuable by respondents, global EET research indicates that, like EET programs themselves, such services represent a heterogeneous category and have shown mixed results. Within the body of research, it is challenging to parse out and isolate the relative value of a specific wrap-around service. Further, these additional elements of EET programs can be expensive components of programs. Nonetheless, among entrepreneurs in the case countries, and beyond facing a number of constraints, the desire to complement knowledge and skill acquisition with additional supports is understandable. This may be reflected in the growing interest in the region in incubator models that embed EET programs within a broader offering of support services for potential entrepreneurs, such as office facilities, Internet access, and meeting space. While not necessarily offering direct access to finance, incubator models serve a segment of entrepreneurs by offering a sense of legitimacy and formality to a business concept, which can better position it for funding and growth.

In Ghana, the Meltwater Entrepreneurial School of Technology, also known as MEST, is attached to the MEST incubator program to provide an ecosystem of training, investment, and mentoring for potential technology entrepreneurs. The program selects potential entrepreneurs from a pool of university graduates to receive comprehensive training in business, computer programming, software development, product management, finance, marketing, sales, and leadership. After completing the two-year intensive program, participants pitch a concept for a business, and the winning teams receive seed funding and a place in the coworking space in the MEST incubator for 18 months to pursue their idea. There they are paired with advisors and mentors, who provide feedback and guidance in the business building process. While this program is only in the fifth year of a 10-year pilot, early signals are positive. For example, GenKey, a leading Ghanaian provider of biometric ID management solutions, recently acquired ClaimSync, one of the firms in MEST's incubator, which provides software that offers hospitals and insurers a next-generation platform for digitizing and processing medical records and claims.

A number of business incubators are also active in Kenya, where they have emerged in two waves: more general programs emerged during the first half of the last decade, and sector-specific incubators have emerged more recently, targeting tech or mobile phone-based business ideas, the arts, or green/climate technologies. The business incubators in Kenya tend to target the segment of growth-oriented business start-ups, that is, innovating university graduates, dynamic technology developers, and others. However, some incubators target unemployed youth (for example, the Urban Entrepreneurship Program, Vijanana Biashara), offering access free of charge (such as through iHub). Only a few incubators offer more structured and systematic start-up support, although it appears that the number of initiatives that aim at venturing into more comprehensive service packages is growing. Growth Africa, a front-runner in the incubator landscape in Kenya, provides structured business training and facilitates venture capital alongside the more common incubator services.

Nonetheless, while incubator models by nature tend to be selective and target the high growth potential segment of entrepreneurs, there are also examples of promising programs that use comprehensive approaches while targeting other types of entrepreneurs. Programs from Mozambique and Kenya demonstrate comprehensive approaches to helping practicing entrepreneurs develop market and supply chain linkages. The International Financial Corporation (IFC) is supporting a three-year program in Mozambique to help small and medium enterprises (SMEs) tap into opportunities from the country's influx of large, capital-intensive industrial projects. Mozlink II (Mozambique SME Linkage Development Program), which began in October 2006, builds the entrepreneurial and managerial competencies, as well as technical capabilities, of practicing entrepreneurs to effectively integrate with the supply chain needs of industrial projects. The Mozlink program covers different features of coaching/mentoring, workshop training, and business networking as well as other services. Since it started, it has generated the following results: (i) 75 SMEs participated in the capacity building training, which focuses on management and technical skills improvement, including a wellness component that ensures that SMEs are aware of best practices to reduce the risk that human immunodeficiency virus (HIV)/acquired immune deficiency syndrome (AIDS), tuberculosis, and malaria pose to their employees and surrounding communities; (ii) more than 3,000 employees were impacted by the program; (iii) more than US$20 million in revenues to SMEs were generated by Mozlink corporate partners to date; (iv) International Finance Corporation (IFC)'s partnership with local banks leveraged access to finance for SMEs; and (v) in 2007–08, new contracts to local SMEs by Mozlink corporate partners grew by 40 percent. While not a rigorous program evaluation, these early results look promising.

Value chain development represents a similar promising approach and has been employed among dairy SMEs in Kenya. Value chain development programs aim to systematically address identified challenges and barriers in a defined value chain, in most cases agricultural. These include barriers related to the legal and regulatory environment, production techniques, market failures, marketing, and access to finance. The Business Service Market Development Project (BSMDP) program, implemented through and in partnership with a number of Kenyan organizations, including SITE and TechnoServe, addressed value chain constraints by offering training to milk traders and producers. Initial outcomes from the program were promising, with the sector as a whole experiencing growth and evidence of reinvestment in businesses and improved business practices (Baiya and Kithinji 2010).

Note

1. Appendix L provides an overview of program evaluations from Component 1 that are described in this chapter.

CHAPTER 6

Key Findings and Conclusion

This report summarizes findings from the three country case studies concerning the context within which entrepreneurship education and training (EET) programs function, the EET program landscapes, and the perspectives of local EET stakeholders. This concluding chapter first describes the key, high-level findings from across the case studies. It then describes a set of insights intended to inform EET policy and program dialog at multiple levels, guide investment decisions that policymakers and government institutions may make with regard to EET programs, and suggest further research in the EET realm.

Summary of Key Findings

All three case countries exhibit diverse entrepreneurial landscapes
This fact reflects the heterogeneous landscape of EET programs globally. In each country, there are examples of both entrepreneurship education and training programs targeting a range of groups that include secondary education students, higher education students, and potential and practicing entrepreneurs. Further, entrepreneurship training programs target both necessity-driven as well as high-growth potential entrepreneurs, although a comparatively larger number of programs target the former. The EET landscapes in Kenya and Ghana were found to be particularly wide and differentiated. EET was found to be a comparatively newer phenomenon in Ghana and Mozambique compared to Kenya.

Programs in case countries tend to rely upon private and international support
Across the three case countries, private, nongovernmental organizations and development partners provide substantive support for EET programs. In Kenya, this trend was most pronounced, with private organizations dominating the EET landscape. Both in terms of implementation and in funding, there is a high level of involvement by development partners, nongovernmental organizations, and multinational firms. A comparatively larger amount of identified programs in

Ghana and Mozambique involve public entities, but even there most were found
to receive some form of donor or nongovernmental organization support.

There is little coordination across the EET efforts in the case countries

The case studies indicate that EET programs in the case countries are fragment-
ed, and there is little evidence of a specific strategy for entrepreneurship promotion at the regional or national level. Even in the context of Kenya, where EE has
been notably integrated within the secondary and postsecondary education system, there is little connection or coordination between programs at these levels.
Interviewees and focus group respondents indicated that there is a strong need
to promote dialog among EET programs and operators, an issue that has been
raised within global EET research as well.

Program landscapes suggest that EET is designed to respond to key contextual challenges

Global EET research indicates that programs seek to address a number of pressing economic imperatives, ranging from employment creation to poverty reduction and innovation. In the case countries, EET was found to be particularly
concerned with employment creation, with each country facing considerably
severe youth unemployment challenges. However, there is little information to
support the role of EET programs in addressing this challenge through the creation of either self-employment or the establishment of enterprises with growth
and formal employment potential. There is also evidence that EET is viewed in
the case countries as a means of addressing poverty within vulnerable populations through income generation. In Mozambique, the emergence of EET programs coincided with the country's recovery from the civil war as a means of
generating income for former combatants as well as refugee populations. There
are additional examples of EET programs in Ghana and Kenya targeting the
substantial sector of necessity-driven, often informal enterprises to support
improved business practices. Global EET research indicates that programs have
promise to support both income generation and improved business practice
adoption in certain contexts.

There is a space between what EET programs practice and what local EET stakeholders value

Examining the identified EET programs and the insights of local EET stakeholders, including both successful and failed entrepreneurs and EET program participants, one finds a notable gap between what the stakeholders demands and the
programs deliver.

- *Building mind-sets.* EET stakeholders indicate that amid negative cultural
  biases toward entrepreneurs and challenging entrepreneurship environments,
  there is a need to focus on building entrepreneurial awareness and
  socio-emotional skills to navigate this context. While identified EET programs

did seek to build awareness of entrepreneurship as an option, little information was found about EET programs in case countries looking to develop socio-emotional skills associated with entrepreneurship, such as critical thinking and self-efficacy. This absence was most notable among programs targeting secondary and higher education students. Programs in case counties instead tend to focus on building business and management skills, entrepreneurial capabilities that, while valued, in the eyes of program participants are overly theoretical and academic in nature.

- *Exposure to the business community.* EET stakeholders across the case countries indicated a desire for exposure to the business community and entrepreneurs within EET programs. This exposure was desired across EET program characteristics, including in instructors (as primary instructors with experience or as joint instructors), in program content and methods (such as guest lectures, site visits, narrative stories, and experiences of entrepreneurs), and within wrap-around services (as mentors or through networking opportunities). Despite this desire, there are few identified programs that prioritize exposure to entrepreneurs or the business community. This, however, is a broader deficit cited within global EET research as well, and there are also examples across program types of promising programs that prioritize this exposure.

- *Tailored and practice-oriented programs.* Local EET stakeholders that participated in EET programs suggested that many programs tended to mix large, heterogeneous groups of participants of varying ages and educational backgrounds. This critique was particularly prevalent among those participating in large-scale programs aimed to address youth unemployment. Respondents indicated that these programs were unable to address the varying needs of their participants and that programs should conduct needs assessments better to ascertain how best to serve various groups. This feedback was discouraging in light of the number of programs across the case countries that aim to combat youth unemployment. In terms of the content, participants felt that programs were overly theoretical and that they would have benefited from more hands-on, practical training. Relatedly, among the programs receiving more positive feedback are those that are tailored to the needs of entrepreneurs in particular sectors. There are examples of several programs in the case countries that are sponsored (at least in part) by business associations, and these seemed to be comparatively well received.

- *Comprehensive approaches to address business environment constraints and provide continued support.* An analysis of the context in each of the case counties indicates that entrepreneurs in each country face a challenging business environment for starting and sustaining successful enterprises. The insights from local EET stakeholders tended to support this characterization of the environment. In turn, stakeholders desired programs that could help overcome these barriers in a comprehensive way, in particular by providing avenues for accessing finance—one of the oft cited barriers—as well as access to markets.

There are promising examples of programs in the case countries that offer relevant wrap-around services, and in some cases entrepreneurship training is a component of broader efforts aimed at value chain and market integration, or in the form of an incubator model. Another form of desired wrap-around services concerns connections with mentors, coaches, or (at a minimum) follow-up services to ensure that training can take hold. In addition, some programs are directly sponsored by or required on the part of microfinance or commercial banking institutions. On the whole, however, respondents felt that more comprehensive efforts were needed to render EET more responsive to the complexity of local needs as opposed to short, often one-off training programs.

Information on the outcomes for identified programs in case countries is scarce

A low level of monitoring and evaluation in the EET environment is prevalent in all three case study countries. Where evaluation occurs at all, it is considered sufficient to trace the performance of beneficiaries in a rather informal way, and more often than not written reports on the outcomes of the assessments are not available. Many of the programs in which rigorous evaluation is defined as a key component are still new and ongoing, so evaluations have still not been conducted or completed. Without systematic and available evaluations of existing programs, the case studies' analysis of the programs and approaches relied mainly on the interviews that were conducted with program managers, beneficiaries and entrepreneurs. In turn, information on the outcomes for programs within the case countries was scarce and largely anecdotal, based on described program objectives. This scarcity, however, is not limited to the case countries; and has been found to be the norm across the global EET landscape.

Information on the costs for identified programs in case countries is scarce

Across the case countries, there is a paucity of information on the costs and financing of EET programs. This finding is consistent with the broader lack of information on costs and financing of EET programs in global EET research. In several cases, implementing organizations considered this information to be proprietary in nature. In some cases, particularly within EESE and EEHE programs, the costs of EET programs are a function of the institutions responsible for implementation as well as associated principles of cost recovery. In turn, there is little available insight into the cost-effectiveness, suggesting that policy makers and program designers alike should be wary of how expensive EET interventions can be, and the associated implications this has for both scale and relative potential to offer robust wraparound services.

Implications for Program Design and Policy

In light of the aforementioned findings, the case studies do provide some lessons for bringing the EET programs closer to the needs of existing, new, or would-be-entrepreneurs both within the countries of inquiry as well as beyond. Generally, for policymakers and program managers, there are two separate but related questions:

- What can be done to strengthen broader interventions, targeting large segments of the population?
- What can be done to strengthen focused interventions across the spectrum of targeted participants—from unemployed youth and marginalized women to highly educated high growth potential entrepreneurs?

Further, cutting across programs there is a need for improved monitoring and evaluation to determine what works best in particular contexts.

For the broader interventions, an emphasis on building foundational skills and mind-sets is needed

One finding that came up in various contexts across the case studies is the lack of appropriate mechanisms to support entrepreneurship attitudes starting at an early age. There is an apparent need to combat negative perceptions to establish entrepreneurship as a respected (even attractive) career option. Mind-set changes in the wider society are essential to fundamentally change attitudes toward entrepreneurship among the people of each country, and this will require more far-reaching interventions that go beyond individual EET programs. Such an approach could provide exposure to positive role models of entrepreneurship among a broader swath of the population, particularly in countries where entrepreneurship is often associated with the struggles of the self-employed in the informal sectors. Furthermore, a secondary-school entrepreneurship education program's objectives and outcomes may include the provision of socio-emotional skills, described as critical by stakeholders, who see these skills as essential for navigating challenging business environments over a lifetime. Among programs targeting secondary education students, the context demands some government role, at least within public institutions or institutions using national curricula. The broader applicability of socio-emotional skills means such programs would contribute toward a general public good and, therefore, may in turn justify some form of government intervention and support.

For focused interventions, greater clarity is needed regarding both target groups and program objectives to foster more tailored programs.

A key finding from the case studies is that programs often bring together large, heterogeneous groups of individuals that render it challenging to meet participants' diverse needs. Clarity about the specific target group, for example whether a program is targeting necessity-driven or high-growth-potential practicing entrepreneurs, and clarity about their associated characteristics (age, educational background) should inform program design. This can help identify which wrap-around services are most appropriate and desired, based on an assessment of the target group's needs. It can also inform how best to blend content to achieve the right balance of business and management training with hands-on or sector-oriented knowledge. It can inform how programs are delivered, for example whether they are held close to where target groups are living and operating, and whether they are delivered by experienced trainers or teachers (ideally experienced entrepreneurs) who speak the language of the beneficiaries. Further, it can inform the duration of training—with some programs, for example, needing to be adjusted to meet the time constraints of practicing entrepreneurs. Examples of this last type from the case countries are training programs run by business associations, providing short just-in-time training to entrepreneurs while also offering a sustainable support network. From a policy standpoint, however, it must be acknowledged that such tailored programs can be expensive, and the cost/benefit use of public resources should be considered in light of other, potentially more appropriate policy options to support particular groups of potential and practicing entrepreneurs in light of the desired policy objectives.

For focused interventions, there is need for more, careful information as to how EET can best support high-growth potential entrepreneurs.

In the case countries, the lack of modern wage jobs and high structural unemployment, particularly for youth, contribute to the large percentage of individuals employed in each countries informal sector. For many, necessity-driven entrepreneurship in the informal sector is an option of last resort; while at best, for those with potential to grow their enterprises, the lack of formalization fosters insecurity as well as legal and financial impediments to growth. Reflecting this challenge, relatively few programs in the case countries focus on supporting potential high growth entrepreneurs, despite the potential spillovers for fostering wage employment. There are examples of incubator models in the case countries that target high-growth-potential individuals, but these programs are selective and relatively little is yet known about how their training components contribute to their participants' subsequent decisions to launch enterprises and succeed as entrepreneurs. Further, such programs for high-growth potential entrepreneurs merit further discussion about government involvement. While the objectives of these programs also tend to align with the interest of governments—including economic spillovers such as employment and innovation—these programs tend to target better educated and better-off individuals, groups for which there is limited rationale for government support. Furthermore, the government role with these sorts of programs is complicated by the perception of "picking winners" as well as practical limitations in identifying "the right" participants, roles that the market and investors are likely better equipped to fill. Thus, for programs targeting high-growth-potential entrepreneurs, the government's role ought to be limited to creating the space for the financing, providing private entities to train, such as business associations, fostering a business environment that enables entrepreneurial activity, including business registration, access to finance, and accommodative tax policies.

For all programs, more monitoring and evaluation of EET programs is needed to inform what works across various contexts.
The case studies indicate that to inform the effectiveness of EET interventions, there is a clear need to design programs with specific measurable goals to assess. Data need to be collected at baseline and in follow-ups. At a minimum, there should be a control group and one or more treatment groups. Ideally, interventions would include randomized controlled trials in their designs so that impacts could be measured. These steps would allow a more rigorous evaluation of effectiveness and impact and should drive better investments and program design going forward. While most EET programs attempt at least some rudimentary program evaluation to assess learning and competencies acquired, postprogram follow-up and rigorous evaluation methods are for the most part absent in the overall program design in all three case study countries (and beyond). While this lack of rigor in program evaluation is troubling, it also provides an opportunity to create an agenda for best practices in program design and evaluation going forward. Such information would offer program designers and policymakers an opportunity to understand what choices are most common for particular target groups, particular outcomes, and within particular contexts.
Finally, the case studies produced a set of specific recommendations that flowed specifically from the perspectives of local EET stakeholders. These recommendations were directed at EET providers in the case countries:

- Conduct a thorough needs assessment during the selection of program participants and group participants according to their level of experience, their knowledge and skills, and the business sector they represent. Tailor the level of training and content based on the participants' needs assessments and selection.
- Improve the quality of trainers in programs by selecting individuals with actual business and entrepreneurship experience and providing them with opportunities to take part in yearly training-of-trainers courses aimed at updating training methodology and technical content.
- Establish a dialog with other EET providers in your region to engage in strategic collaboration regarding the provision of training and wrap-around services.
- Make the entrepreneurship education or training curriculum practical and experiential, involving local entrepreneurs and business owners as guest lecturers and mentors.
- Highlight and connect participants with successful entrepreneurs to serve as role models within all programs.

Conclusion

The case studies indicate that potential and practicing entrepreneurs in Ghana, Kenya, and Mozambique have reason for optimism with regard to the expansion of entrepreneurial opportunity. All three countries are experiencing periods of sustained economic growth, a diversifying private sector, and a less capital-intensive services sector becoming an increasingly dominant contributor to each country's economy. Nonetheless, entrepreneurs in the case countries indicated that they face considerable barriers to success. Several of these cited barriers, including corruption, bureaucratic red-tape, and lack of access to finance, are beyond the scope of EET interventions, which aim to support entrepreneurship through the provision of knowledge and skills. In turn, the case studies indicate that EET is not viewed, nor should it be viewed, as a panacea to these challenges. However, the case studies indicate that insufficient knowledge and skills are a persistent barrier for potential and practicing entrepreneurs alike and that EET can be of value for entrepreneurs of all types in the near and medium term, particularly for strengthening business practices, integrating into new markets, and building networks. Further, over the long term, increasing awareness of entrepreneurship early on through the education system is viewed as a means of developing foundational, transferable socioemotional skills, combating negative perceptions, and leveling the playing field by offering exposure to entrepreneurship as a means of economic mobility for those without it through parents and peers.

The case studies summarized in this report are designed to inform a broader understanding of how EET programs are contributing to addressing entrepreneurial barriers in three particular countries. This has enabled a unique contextualized look at EET that complements global research as well as individual evaluations at specific programs. The countries' pressing economic imperatives, ranging from employment creation to poverty reduction and innovation, are national in scope, and EET programs, while rarely coordinated within a country, do operate within a national and regional context. Thus, looking at the EET landscape from this perspective can provide useful insights for policymakers and program designers alike. The findings from the case studies, which identify a range of EET programs within each of the case countries, also suggest that there is a need for more dialogue among EET programs and operators, not only to avoid duplication and the inefficient use of resources, but also to promote cross-program learning regarding emerging practices. Such information, through associated efforts to measure the outcomes of EET programs, will contribute to the growing national, regional, and global understanding of the value of EET in light of its promise to meet ambitious objectives.

Program Landscape in Ghana

Program Type	Program Name
Entrepreneurship Education: Secondary Education Students	Career Development and Entrepreneurship Programme
	Entrepreneurship Skills Training (offered in all GES Technical and Vocational Institutes)
	School Enterprise Project
	Business Boot Camp
Entrepreneurship Education: Higher Education Students	BSc Entrepreneurship (Ghana Institute of Management and Public Administration)
	BSc Entrepreneurship (Entrepreneurship Training Institute)
	Massachusetts Institute of Technology Accelerating Information Technology Innovation (MIT AITI)
	Higher National Diploma in Entrepreneurship and Finance (Kumasi Polytechnic)
	Bachelor of Business Administration in Entrepreneurship (Ghana Baptist University College)
	MBA in Entrepreneurship and Small Business Management (KNUST School of Business, Kwame Nkrumah University of Science and Tech)
	Entrepreneurship Clinic for final year undergraduates (KNUST School of Business, Kwame Nkrumah University of Science and Tech)
	Entrepreneurship Capstone Course (Ashesi University College)
	Entrepreneurship Development (University of Professional Studies, Accra)
	Entrepreneurship Course (University of Ghana Business School)
	Takoradi Polytechnic
	Entrepreneurship course (Cape Coast Polytechnic)
	MBA Entrepreneurship and Small Enterprise Development (University of Cape Coast)
	MCom Entrepreneurship and Small Enterprise Development (University of Cape Coast)

table continues next page

Program Type	Program Name
Entrepreneurship Training: Potential Entrepreneurs	Business & Entrepreneur Development Centre (BEDeC)
	Creative Enterprise Training (CET) Programme
	Training of Youth in Aquaculture
	Vocational Training for Women Programme
	Meltwater Entrepreneurial School of Technology
	Entrepreneurial Skills—Opportunities Industrialization Centers Ghana (OIC Ghana)
	Entrepreneurship Training Workshop (Empretec Ghana Foundation)
	Believe Begin Become
	Entrepreneurship Course (Institute of Directors)
	Business Launch-Pad
	Local Enterprises and Skill Development (LESDEP)
	Ghana Youth Enterprise and Entrepreneurial Devpt. Agency (GYEEDA)
	National Youth Employment Programme
	Start-up West Africa
Entrepreneurship Training: Practicing Entrepreneurs	Certificate in Entrepreneurship/Small Business Management
	Certificate in Entrepreneurial Management (CEM)
	Rural Enterprises Programme
	Suame Magazine Industrial Development Organization (SMIDO)
	E-Circle
	Sustaining Competitive and Responsible Enterprises (SCORE)
	Enablis Entrepreneurial Network
	Business Development Centre
	Sound Financial Management for Women Entrepreneurs

Source: World Bank.

Program Landscape in Kenya

Program Type	Program Name
Entrepreneurship Education: Secondary Education Students	Entrepreneurship Education in TIVET
	Business Studies/ Education in Adult Basic Education and Training (ABET)
	Entrepreneurship in NF Basic Education
	Business Studies in secondary education
Entrepreneurship Education: Higher Education Students	Practical Entrepreneurship Training (Regional Center for Enterprise Development, Inoorero University)
	Student Training for Entrepreneurship Promotion, Kenyatta University
	Chandaria Incubation and Innovation Center, Kenyatta University
	Global Business School Network
	Strathmore Enterprise & Development Centre (Strathmore University)
Entrepreneurship Training: Potential Entrepreneurs	Slumidia
	Kenya Youth Empowerment and Employment Initiative (KYEEI)
	Young Enterprise Development Fund (YEDF)
	Kenya Climate Innovation Centre
	Grofin
	VijananaBiashara
	Start-up!
	5by20
	m:lab
	Nailab
	Savannah Fund
	Bid network
	NairoBits
	Jitihada Business Plan Competition
	KYBT (Kenya Youth Business Trust) Mombasa
	Young Women in Enterprise, TechnoServe
	STRYDE, TechnoServe
	Yes, Youth Can! TechnoServe
	ilab Africa Research Institute
	IU- MSME Mentorship Program

table continues next page

Program Type	Program Name
Entrepreneurship Training: Practicing Entrepreneurs	Kenya Institute of Business Training [KIBT]
	SME Business Training, Clinics & Coaching
	Entrepreneurship and Money
	Fanikisha Initiative
	Enablis
	SME Toolkit Training for Entrepreneurial Development
	Samsung Real Dreams
	JuhudiKilimo
	OVOP (One Village One Product)
	88 mph
	KuzaBiashara
	Yehu
	KAWBO

Source: World Bank.

Program Landscape in Mozambique

Program Type	Program Name
Entrepreneurship Education: Secondary Education Students	DNET—Entrepreneurship Modules in Professional and Technical schools
	PIREP—Technical and Vocational Education Reform Project
	MINED—Entrepreneurship education
Entrepreneurship Education: Higher Education Students	UP/ESTEC—Entrepreneurship courses
	Empresa Junior/ISCTEM
	ESNEC—Business and Entrepreneurship Higher Ed. School in Chibuto
	Business Management (UEM)
Entrepreneurship Training: Potential Entrepreneurs	NEC and Gestão de PMEs
	Pro-Jovem
	Fundo de Desenvolvimento Distrital (FDD)
	ILO Comece o seu Negócio and Desenvolva o seu negócio
	INEFP—Professional Training Centres
	Aga Khan Foundation—EDI Cabo Delgado
	Internet Solutions—IS
	ESSOR
	RIC/ISPM—Research and Incubation Center
	ACIANA—Industrial and Agricultural Association
	GAPI Youth Entrepreneurship Program
	IAC—Chimoio Agricultural Institute—CSDC
Entrepreneurship Training: Practicing Entrepreneurs	Institute for the Promotion of Small and Medium-Sized Enterprises (IPEME)
	Programme of Cooperation in Science, Technology and Innovation between Finland and Mozambique (STIFIMO)
	Investment and financing company (GAPI)
	MOZLINK
	Institute for Export Promotion (IPEX)
	USAID—Technoserve
	NegóciosInclusivos
	Support to Competitiveness and Enterprise Development Project (PACDE)

Source: World Bank.

Survey Questions for Qualitative Interviews: Program Managers

1) *Program Design and Evaluation*
- What are the goals of the entrepreneurship education (EE)/entrepreneurship training (ET) program?
- What are the specific objectives that can be tracked that measure the success of fulfilling the mission and meeting the goals of the program?
- What are the needs and abilities of the target program participants and how do you select the program participants?

2) *Trainers and Delivery*
- How would you describe the background of the trainers/instructors of the entrepreneurial education and training (EET) program? (examples: practitioners, college professors, vocational trainers) and do you provide them any training or development opportunities?
- How did you select the manner in which the curriculum is delivered? (examples: hands on/experiential, lectures, reading assignments, web assignments, small groups, one on one instruction)?

3) *Content and Curriculum*
- Does the content link theoretical concepts to real-world experiences? If so, how?
- Is the content adapted to the context in which the program participants operate? If so, how?
- Do practitioners/existing entrepreneurs interact with program participants? If so, how?
- What knowledge/skills are covered in the program and how are they prioritized?
  - Critical thinking, decision making, problem solving, creative thought
  - General Business Skills: management, marketing, customer identification, production/service delivery, sales, human resources

- Financial Skills: accounting, budgeting, financing and capital structure
- Soft Skills: communication, leadership, negotiation, presentation.

4) *Wrap Around Services*

- What kinds of wrap-around services are offered to program participants? (examples: networking events, mentoring, community linkages, financial capital, technology, markets, office space)
- What kinds, if any, of postprogram support do you offer?

5) *Other*

- How do you determine if you are successful in meeting the goals and objectives of the EET program?
- What are the most significant barriers to generating more high growth entrepreneurship in this country?
- Are EET programs effectively addressing these barriers?
- Open ended: Is there anything else you'd like to comment on regarding EET or the entrepreneurial ecosystem in your country?

Survey Questions for Qualitative Interviews: Successful Entrepreneurs

1) *Profile*

   Name, age, gender, nationality, education, years of industry experience, previous start-up experience (number and outcomes of previous businesses)

2) *Questions about current business (or main business if respondent owns more than one)*
   - In what year did you start the business?
   - What industry sector is the business in?
   - Did you have co-founders (if so, how many)?
   - How many employees do you currently have?
   - What was the annual turnover (revenues) in 2012?
   - Was the firm profitable in 2012?
   - What is the most significant challenge facing your business in 2013?
   - How would you describe the entrepreneurial ecosystem in this country?
   - Did you take part in any entrepreneurial education and training (EET) programs before or while you were starting this business?

3) *If yes:*
   - What was the program(s)?
   - How long was the program and how was the curriculum delivered?
   - What were the most valuable elements?
   - What kinds of wrap around services were offered to program participants? (examples: networking events, mentoring, community linkages, financial capital, technology, markets, office space)
   - What were the most valuable services?
   - What kinds, if any, of post program support were offered?
   - What were the most valuable types of support?
   - How would you define successful entrepreneurship and would you describe yourself as a successful entrepreneur?

- What are the most significant barriers to starting and growing your business in this country?
- Are EET programs effectively addressing these barriers?
- Open ended: Is there anything else you'd like to comment on regarding EET or the entrepreneurial ecosystem in your country?

Focus Group Instrument: Failed/Discouraged Entrepreneurs

- What were your goals in participating in an entrepreneurial education and training (EET) program? What did you expect or hope to accomplish from your participation?
- How would you describe the background of the trainers/instructors of the EET program and did you feel they were effective in teaching the curriculum? (examples: practitioners, college professors, vocational trainers)
- How effective was the manner in which the curriculum was delivered and would you have preferred another manner? (examples: hands on/experiential, lectures, reading assignments, web assignments, small groups, one on one instruction)
- Did the content link theoretical concepts to real world experiences?
- Was the content adapted to the context in which you would operate a business?
- Was there interaction between you and practitioners/existing entrepreneurs?
- What knowledge/skills were covered in the program that you felt were valuable?
  - Critical thinking, decision-making, problem solving, creative thought
  - General Business Skills: management, marketing, customer identification, production/service delivery, sales, human resources
  - Financial Skills: accounting, budgeting, financing and capital structure
  - Soft Skills: communication, leadership, negotiation, presentation.
- What knowledge/skills were covered in the program that you felt were not valuable?
- What kinds of wrap around services are offered to program participants (examples: networking events, mentoring, community linkages, financial capital, technology, markets, office space) and which ones did you feel were most valuable?

- What kinds of post program support were offered? Did you take advantage of them?
- If you started a business and it didn't survive—what do you feel were the major reasons why the business did not succeed?
- If you decided not to start a business—what were the major reasons why you chose not to start a business?
- What are the most significant barriers to generating more high growth entrepreneurship in this country?
- Are EET programs effectively addressing these barriers?
- Open ended: Is there anything else you'd like to comment on regarding EET or the entrepreneurial ecosystem in your country?

Focus Group Instrument: Program Participants/Potential Entrepreneurs

- What were your goals in participating in an entrepreneurial education and training (EET) program? What did you expect or hope to accomplish from your participation?
- How would you describe the background of the trainers/instructors of the EET program and do you feel they were effective in teaching the curriculum? (examples: practitioners, college professors, vocational trainers)
- How effective was the manner in which the curriculum was delivered and would you have preferred another manner? (examples: hands on/experiential, lectures, reading assignments, web assignments, small groups, one on one instruction)
- Did the content link theoretical concepts to real world experiences?
- Was the content adapted to the context in which you would operate a business?
- Was there interaction between you and practitioners/existing entrepreneurs?
- What knowledge/skills were covered in the program that you felt were valuable?
  - Critical thinking, decision-making, problem solving, creative thought
  - General Business Skills: management, marketing, customer identification, production/service delivery, sales, human resources
  - Financial Skills: accounting, budgeting, financing and capital structure
  - Soft Skills: communication, leadership, negotiation, presentation.
- What knowledge/skills were covered in the program that you felt were not valuable?
- What kinds of wrap around services are offered to program participants (examples: networking events, mentoring, community linkages, financial capital, technology, markets, office space) and which ones did you feel were most valuable?
- What kinds of post program support were offered? Did you take advantage of them?

- Do you think you will start a business in the next year or sometime in the future?
- If yes, what kind of growth aspirations do you have? (one person-self-employment, generate employment for 1 to 4 people, generate employment 5 to 24 people, generate employment for 25 to 50 people, generate employment for more than 50 people).
- What are the most significant barriers to generating more high growth entrepreneurship in this country?
- Are EET programs effectively addressing these barriers?
- Open ended: Is there anything else you'd like to comment on regarding EET or the entrepreneurial ecosystem in your country?

Focus Group Instrument: Program Participants/Practicing Entrepreneurs

- What were your goals in participating in an entrepreneurial education and training (EET) program? What did you expect or hope to accomplish from your participation?
- How would you describe the background of the trainers/instructors of the EET program and do you feel they were effective in teaching the curriculum? (examples: practitioners, college professors, vocational trainers)
- How effective was the manner in which the curriculum was delivered and would you have preferred another manner? (examples: hands on/experiential, lectures, reading assignments, web assignments, small groups, one on one instruction)
- Did the content link theoretical concepts to real world experiences?
- Was the content adapted to the context in which you would operate a business?
- Was there interaction between you and practitioners/existing entrepreneurs?
- What knowledge/skills were covered in the program that you felt were valuable?
  - Critical thinking, decision-making, problem solving, creative thought
  - General Business Skills: management, marketing, customer identification, production/service delivery, sales, human resources
  - Financial Skills: accounting, budgeting, financing and capital structure
  - Soft Skills: communication, leadership, negotiation, presentation.
- What knowledge/skills were covered in the program that you felt were not valuable?
- What kinds of wrap around services are offered to program participants (examples: networking events, mentoring, community linkages, financial capital, technology, markets, office space) and which ones did you feel were most valuable?
- What kinds, if any, of post program support were offered to you? Did you take advantage of them?

- What kind of growth aspirations do you have for your business? (one person-self-employment, generate employment for 1 to 4 people, generate employment 5 to 24 people, generate employment for 25 to 50 people, generate employment for more than 50 people).
- What are the most significant barriers to generating more high growth entrepreneurship?
- Are EET programs effectively addressing these barriers?
- Open ended: Is there anything else you'd like to comment on regarding EET or the entrepreneurial ecosystem in your country?

Focus Groups and Interviews in Ghana

Focus groups			
Type of group	*Program attended (if relevant)*	*Location*	*Number (female/male)*
Potential	Fundamentals of Entrepreneurship	UGBS Accra	8 (4/4)
Potential	Fundamentals of Entrepreneurship	KNUST Kumasi	6 (2/4)
Potential	BSc. in Entrepreneurship	ETI Accra	8 (4/4)
Potential	Technical training with entrepreneurship	ATTC, Accra	7 (1/6)
Practicing	MEST	MEST, Accra	8 (4/4)
Practicing	Postgrad dip in Entrepreneurship	ETI Accra	5 (1/4)
Practicing	Spinnet	Spinnet, Accra	6 (4/2)
Practicing	Vocational training for Females	VTF, Accra	7 (7/0)
Interviews with successful entrepreneurs			
Name	*Sector (company)*	*Location*	*Background*
J.S. Addo	Banking (Prudential Bank)	Accra	Business degree in economics
Dr. Michael A. Addo	Pharmaceutical (KAMA group of companies)	Accra	BSc. in pharmacy, MA in industrial management
Eunice Ijeoma Aku Ogbugo	Engineering design and construction (EugoTerrano)	Accra	BSc. civil engineering
E.J. Villars	Printing (Camelot)	Accra	G.C.E—O Level
Patrick Fares	Hotels/real estate (Holiday Inn)	Accra	Bachelor's degree; 2 MBAs (management/ contracts & acquisitions)
Ellen Hagan	Human resource Consulting (L'Aine)	Accra	MBA in industrial relations

Interviews with program managers
Program name
Program in Entrepreneurship (University of Ghana Business School)
BSc. in Entrepreneurship (Entrepreneurship Training Institute)
Post-graduate Diploma in Entrepreneurship (Entrepreneurship Training Institute)
Enterprise Development Service (University of Ghana Business School)
National Board for Small Scale Industries
MEST
Vocational Training For Women
Auto-Diagnostics in Computer training (Suame Magazine Industrial Development Organization (SMIDO))
Technical training (National Vocational Training Institute)
Program in Entrepreneurship (University of Professional Studies Accra (UPSA)

Source: World Bank.

Focus Groups and Interviews in Kenya

Focus groups			
Type of group	Program attended (if relevant)	Location	Number (female/male)
Potential	Mlab	Nairobi	9 (3/6)
Potential	Junior Achievement	Mombasa	
Potential	MOYAS	Malindi	14 (5/9)
Practicing	KYBT	Mombasa	6 (3/3)
Practicing	JKUAT Degree	Nairobi	7 (2/5)
Failed/discouraged	YWE/Technoserve	Kawangare/Nairobi	7 (7/0)—age 23–26
Failed/discouraged	YWE/Technoserve	Kawangare/Nairobi	6 (6/0)—age 17–21
Failed/discouraged	YWE (5by20)/ Technoserve	Kariobangi/Nairobi	6 (6/0)—teenagers
Failed/discouraged	YWE (5by20)/Technoserve	Kariobangi/Nairobi	7 (7/0)—adults
Interviews with successful entrepreneurs			
Name	Sector (company)	Location	Background
Laura Akunga	Business Services (Benchmark Solutions)	Nairobi	Business degree and short further training
Mercy Obukwa	Art (Art-Folio)	Nairobi	Chandaria Incubator/KU
Mr. Julius Mburugu	Consultancy, business services (Entwise Associates)	Nairobi	Degree Entrepreneurship from UK university
Thomas Kimani Njeru	Entertainment (KIZZY Clowns Entertainment)	Nairobi	KIM, KYBT
Anna Karwitha and Anna Kunstmaler	Tourism (Safaris)	Mombasa	KuzaBiashara
James Maina	Mawa Dairy	Mombasa	ADB
Simon Gicharu	Education (Mount Kenya University)	Thika	ET from British Council and Cranfield University

Interviews with program managers
Program name
Yes Youth Can
STRYDE (Strengthening Rural Youth Development through Enterprise (*STRYDE*)
KuzaBiashara
YEHU
STEP (Chandaria Business Innovation and Incubation Centre)
Entrepreneurship and Handicraft for Export, Supplier Diversifying Program
ADB (African Development Bank)
KYBT (Kenya Youth Business Trust)
CEED (Centre for Entrepreneurship & Enterprise Development (*CEED*)
Entrepreneurship training (Young Entrepreneurs Association Nyahururu)
Growth Africa
Degree in Entrepreneurship (Jomo Kenyatta University of Agriculture and Technology)
Youth Empowerment Centers (MOYAS)
Entrepreneurship and Business Studies in general education (Ministry of Education); Ministry of Higher Education, Science and Technology [MoHEST])
Mentorship training (Kenyatta University)
KAB

Source: World Bank.

Focus Groups and Interviews in Mozambique

Focus groups			
Type of group	Program attended (if relevant)	Location	Number (female/male)
Failed/discouraged		Maputo	5 (2/3)
Practicing		Nampula	17
Practicing		Manica	15 (1/14)
Practicing		Maputo	8 (3/5
Potential	Manica High Polytechnic School	Manica	5 (0/5)
Potential	Eduardo Mondlane University	Maputo	19 (8/11)
EET trainers		Nampula	2 (1/1)
EET trainers	Secondary school teachers; Chimoio Agricultural Institute; Industrial and Commerce School; and Manica Province education managers	Manica	9 (1/8)
EET trainers	INEFP, ESSOR, PIREP	Maputo	20 (5/15)
Interviews with successful entrepreneurs			
Number (female/male)	Sector (company)	Location	
3 (1/2)	Agriculture	Nampula	
7 (2/5)	Construction, Agriculture	Manica	
2 (1/1)	Manufacturing		

Interviews with program managers
Program name
Associação Comercial e Industrial de Nampula
Associação de Artesãos de Nampula
Associação de Mulheres Empresarias—ACTIVA Nampula
Manica Polytechnic Institute
Chimoio Agricultural Institute
DNET
PIREP
UP/ESTEC
CTA
IPEME
STIFIMO
PROCESS
MOZLINK
PUM
OIT
e-REVOLUTION
IS
PACDE
UNIDO
Association of Micro Importers from Mozambique
Association of Operators and Workers of the Informal sector

Source: World Bank.

EET Programs Cited from *EET Dimensions for Success*

Entrepreneurship Education—Secondary Education Students (EESE)

Program name	Program beneficiaries	Evaluation	Sample	Outcomes measured	Key findings
BizWorld | **The Netherlands** | *Source:* Huber, Sloof, and van Praag 2012	Children in the final grades of primary school	Randomized field experiment	The sample consisted of 85 schools (the universe was 113 schools that had signed up for the program in 2010 and 2011, out of which 75 percent consented to participating in the research)—a total of 118 classes and 2,751 students in the last year of primary school. The response rate was 87.7 percent. Because the program was delivered at this class level, the unit of analysis was class level rather than school level. Schools and classes were assigned to a treatment or a control group. For both groups, the study applied a pretest/posttest design to allow an unbiased difference-in-differences estimate of the nontreatment effect.	Direct (short-term) effect of early entrepreneurship education on the development of (a) noncognitive skills including self-efficacy, need for achievement, risk taking, social orientation, persistence, motivating, analyzing, proactivity, and creativity; (b) cognitive skills, including entrepreneurship knowledge; and (c) entrepreneurial intentions, including children's intentions to become entrepreneurs.	• The treatment effect was positive and statistically significant for seven of the nine noncognitive skills tested, namely self-efficacy (0.149***), need for achievement (0.166***), risk taking propensity (0.114**), persistence (0.105**), analyzing (0.127***), creativity (0.096*), and proactivity (0.144***). Analysis on the heterogeneity of treatment effects showed that the treatment effects remained or increased slightly when controlling for individual, school, and neighborhood characteristics and year of data collection. Also, the size of treatment effects was substantial and comparable to being eligible to one track level in entering high school (i.e., from the baseline of prevocational to general secondary education). • The estimated effect on cognitive entrepreneurial skills (entrepreneurship knowledge) was positive although not significant (0.015). • The estimated effect on entrepreneurial intentions (to own a business) for children was negative and significant (−0.134***). The study acknowledged that the measures used for entrepreneurial intentions were not validated for children and could potentially alter the results.

table continues next page

Program name	Program beneficiaries	Evaluation	Sample	Outcomes measured	Key findings
NFTE | Network for Teaching Entrepreneurship | **United States** *Source:* Nakkula et al. 2004.	High school students (currently in 18 high schools) in Boston. The program targets high schools where at least half of the student body is eligible for free or reduced-priced lunch.	Quasi-experimental design	The sample included a total of 17 classrooms, 13 teachers and 268 students, out of which 158 students received the NFTE program (treatment) and 110 students were selected in the comparison classes (control).	Entrepreneurship thinking; entrepreneurial behavior through an entrepreneurial activities checklist (49 activities organized around different domains and dimensions); locus of control. Applied new scales to measure healthy or positive development (using the values in action scale that gauges originality, curiosity, industriousness, and hopefulness).	• Entrepreneurial behavior increased for NFTE students compared to the control group. The entrepreneurial behavior score for NFTE students registered a significant increase of 7.5 percent ($p < .01$). The changes in the two groups were large and significant for the starter dimension and business domain. • In contrast, the entrepreneurial behavior score for comparison students did not register significant changes, although in some domains the trend declined. • Although the results for locus of control were not significant, the scores followed the hypothesized pattern. While NFTE students began with marginally lower locus of control scores than the comparison group, they increased their score by about 3 percent after the intervention, outscoring the control group. Similarly, immigrant students participating in the program improved in their locus of control by about 4.5 percent while the score of similar students in the comparison group declined by approximately 2.5 percent. • Locus of control findings were strongest for students taught by one particular teacher in one of the schools with a strong track record of effective teaching (i.e., had received recognition). • Results on students' connectedness were generally negative. • Results from the values in action scales (originality, curiosity, industriousness and hopefulness) were not found to be significant. Despite this, NFTE students scored marginally higher than the comparison group in the pretest; meanwhile, the gap narrowed at posttest with the comparison group increasing their score and the NFTE students decreasing the score. • Overall, NFTE students trained by top-notch teachers showed a higher degree of general student teacher connectedness, unlike the comparison group. • Similar to the findings from the first phase, relative to the comparison group, NFTE students expressed increasingly strong interest in occupations requiring advanced training or formal education, including college.

table continues next page

Entrepreneurship Education—Secondary Education Students (EESE)

Program name	Program beneficiaries	Evaluation	Sample	Outcomes measured	Key findings
INJAZ | Junior Achievement **Morocco, Lebanon, Jordan, Saudi, United Arab Emirates and Egypt, Arab Rep.** Source: Reimers, Dyer, and Ortega 2012[a]	Students in upper secondary that participated in the INJAZ Company Program	Tier 2 | Quasi-experimental design	The pool of students came from a small number of cities in the six countries. Its total size was 1,454 students, of whom 617 were interviewed for the baseline of the comparison group and 837 for the treatment group. Students were not randomly assigned to either group, and because of limitations in implementation, researchers could only match pre- and postsurveys in limited cases. (The baseline questionnaire was collected in December 2010 and January 2011, and the follow-up survey was collected in July and November 2011.)	Student knowledge, skills and attitudes, and behavioral intentions about entrepreneurship.	• Participants in the Junior Achievement programs had very high levels of access to entrepreneurs in their lives. Around 80 percent had siblings who were entrepreneurs, and 30 to 74 percent indicated that their parents or neighbors were entrepreneurs. • They had medium levels of knowledge of basic entrepreneurial concepts. • They had high and positive aspirations, views of self and others, self-efficacy and interest in business creation. • They had favorable attitudes toward entrepreneurship and business.
JAN | Junior Achievement | **Namibia** Source: Mahohoma, E., and M. Muyambo. 2008.	Upper secondary level students in Namibian schools	Qualitative and quantitative analysis through structured questionnaires.	The scope of the study was six regions in Namibia; gathering information of parents, teachers and learners from randomly selected schools from each region. In total, 13 schools participated, including 13 teachers, 130 learners and 90 parents.	The study's objective was to appraise the impact of entrepreneurship education among Namibian youth in areas of entrepreneurship, financial literacy and work-related life skills acquisition. The outcomes were assessed in terms of entrepreneurship education, financial literacy and work-related life skills from the teachers, learners and parents' perspective.	• 82 percent of the teachers acknowledged that students were learning entrepreneurship abilities, social and financial skills, and employability, as well as responsibility, social involvement and critical thinking. • Parents indicated that benefits from the programs were derived from learning the use of money, budgeting, business-related subjects, intentions, and appreciation skills. Parents also acknowledged helping the students with their own businesses in bookkeeping, start-ups, and business-related needs. • 86 percent of parents indicated that the program led to positive changes in their child's behavior. • 80 percent of students joined the program to learn skills and knowledge on starting their own businesses, and 93 percent confirmed that they learned entrepreneurship abilities, financial literacy and work-related skills. 72 percent indicated a positive impact on their life in the same areas they learned skills.

table continues next page

Entrepreneurship Education—Secondary Education Students (EESE)

Program name	Program beneficiaries	Evaluation	Sample	Outcomes measured	Key findings
SAIE | South African Institute for Entrepreneurship | **South Africa** *Source:* South African Institute for Entrepreneurship 2006	Primary and secondary school students in South Africa	Treatment group (business venture curricula delivered over a period of time) and control group (no intervention). No information on randomization in the assignment to the treatment.	The first evaluation took place in 2003 using a sample of five schools in the greater Cape Town metro area. The second evaluation took place in 2005 using a sample of 41 schools in two provinces.	SAIE aims to influence students' entrepreneurial knowledge, skills, and attitudes by improving the educational process through quality materials and educator training. Started in 1996, SAIE has developed and implemented entrepreneurship education programs in more than 2,500 South African schools. To date, 5,676 schools have implemented the business ventures course. About one-third of the schools are primary schools and two-thirds are secondary schools.	• The 2003 evaluation showed that, compared with a control group, schools implementing the business venture curricula had significant positive effects on students' entrepreneurial knowledge, skills, and attitudes; and. • The 2005 study confirmed the 2003 results but pointed to a picture far more complex than originally thought. The results showed that (i) extraneous factors (socioeconomic profile) were a powerful influence on student performance at time more influential than teaching materials; (ii) entrepreneurial skill acquisition was not a neat, linear process, but proceeded haphazardly over a longer period of time than originally thought—stronger performance improvements were associated with the use of business ventures after a two-year period than with the use of business ventures over a one-year period; and (iii) schools were complex, fluid, and challenging environments for educational interventions; therefore, implementation issues were critical to improving student performance.

Entrepreneurship Education—Higher Education Students (EEHE)

Program name	Program beneficiaries	Evaluation	Sample	Outcomes measured	Key findings
STEP	Student Training for Entrepreneurship Promotion	**Uganda** Source: Gielnick et al. forthcoming	Undergraduate students in their final semester	Randomized controlled field experiment	Students at Makerere University and Uganda Christian University. Among the 651 applications received, 200 were selected to receive the training right away (treatment group) and 200 were placed in a waiting group (control group) that received the training after completion of the study. The data were collected using a pretest/posttest design at three points in time (T1, T2, and T3).	Entrepreneurial self-efficacy, action knowledge, action planning, entrepreneurial goals, entrepreneurial action, business opportunity identification, and business ownership	• Action knowledge was a central factor promoting the initiation and maintenance of entrepreneurial activity. Compared to the control group, the training increased the likelihood of starting a business by 50 percent, and compared to the initial status in the training group, the training increased the likelihood of starting a business by 219 percent. • The training had a positive and significant effect on (a) entrepreneurial self-efficacy ($F = 10.44, p < 0.01$, interaction effect $= .03$ and group effect after training 0.44); (b) action knowledge ($F = 17.65, p < 0.01$, interaction effect $= .05$ and group effect after training 0.61); (c) action planning ($F = 5.53, p < 0.05$, interaction effect $= .02$ and group effect after training 0.47), and business opportunity identification ($F = 7.70, p < .01$, interaction effect $= .02$ and group effect after training 0.42). The effect of training on entrepreneurial goals was marginally supported ($F = 2.88, p < 0.10$, interaction effect $= .01$ and group effect after training 0.31); and. • Entrepreneurial action at T2 had a significant effect on entrepreneurial action at T3 ($\beta = 0.26; p < 0.01$) and action knowledge had a significant and positive effect on entrepreneurial action ($\beta = 0.13; p < 0.05$). The coefficient on entrepreneurial self-efficacy on entrepreneurial action was not significant.
APSB	Auchi Polytechnic School of Business	**Nigeria** Source: Idogho and Ainabor 2011	Tertiary students at Auchi Polytechnic	Quantitative analysis of survey responses. No indication of an experimental design.	The study used a sample of 300 final year tertiary school students who had filled out surveys.	APSB aims to teach students the skills around managing a small-scale business as a way of preparing them for gainful employment after graduating. This is an initiative of the Nigerian federal government to introduce entrepreneurship education programs in tertiary schools. The evaluation assessed the efficacy of entrepreneurship education on their employability.	• A positive correlation was found between entrepreneurship education and managerial skill development; and. • Students who received instruction in entrepreneurship education showed a greater desire to set up small-scale businesses after graduation.

Entrepreneurship Training—Potential Entrepreneurs (ETPo)					
Program name	Program beneficiaries	Evaluation	Sample	Outcomes measured	Key findings
EPAG | Economic Empowerment of Adolescent Girls and Young Women | Liberia Source: World Bank 2012d	About 2,500 beneficiaries in nine communities in Monrovia and Kakata City	Randomized pipeline research design	Approximately 2,500 young women were accepted to participate in the program. The evaluation random-ized participants into two types of treatment groups: (i) training package on business development and life skills; and (ii) training package on job, entrepreneurship and life skills. There was also a control group. Impact was defined as the change in outcomes between the time the program started and six months after the classroom training ended, as compared to a statistically similar control group (the second round trainees).	Employment, behaviors, empowerment and agency, and family welfare.	• The program was well received—the retention rate was 95 percent and attendance averaged 90 percent. • The program increased employment among trainees by 50 percent compared to those in the control group. • Positive employment outcomes were driven primarily by the business development skills trainees, whose monthly income increased by US$75 per month. • The program increased girls' savings compared to the control group. At midline, the treatment group had a total of US$44 more in savings compared to the control group; and. • There were no significant changes to borrowing or lending among beneficiaries.

table continues next page

WINGS	1,800 beneficiaries	Randomized	The sample consisted of 1,800	Earnings, earning oppor-	• A year after the intervention, monthly cash earnings doubled from
[Women's Income Generating Support Program] **Uganda**	(86 percent poor women) in 120 villages across two districts in Northern Uganda	control experiment with mixed-methods data collection	(mostly) poor women ages 14 to 30 from 120 villages (15 beneficiaries per village). The evaluation built a wait-list control group whereby 900 of the beneficiaries were	tunities, distribution of poverty impacts, savings, characteristics of individual success, health (sick days, hunger, health status, index of depression and anxiety),	16,500 to 31,300 Uganda Shillings 31,300 (US$ 6.60 to 12.52), cash savings tripled, and short-term expenditure on goods and services, and durable assets increased 30 to 50 percent relative to the control group (the average treatment effect is 16,200 Uganda Shillings per month and the median treatment effect is 9,700 Uganda Shillings per month).
Source: Blattman et al. 2013			randomized in the program in phase 1 (mid 2009) and another 900 in phase 2 (early 2011). For phase 1, the program evaluation placed the	empowerment (indices of economic decision making, gender attitudes, interpersonal violence, indepen-	• The treatment had the greatest impact on the people with the lowest initial levels of capital and access to credit.
			randomized participants into three groups: one received the WINGs program, another	dence household support), and social capital (groups and networks, trust, social	• Among those who responded to treatment with more economic success (rather than average levels of economic success), the study found that women had lower success and individuals with higher levels of access to credit at baseline saw fewer gains.
			group received the core package plus the cross-cutting design package (support for business networks), and the	cohesion, collective action)	• There was no large positive effect of skills/education, patience or good health on response to treatment.
			last group acted as the wait-listed control group.		• There were few health and social effects (positive or negative) of the intervention on beneficiaries.
					• There was little effect on psychological or social well-being from the observed reduction in poverty.
					• There was no effect found on women's independence, status in the community, or freedom from intimate- partner violence.
					• Involving male partners and training the couples brought more positive results on the couples' interactions and on women's physical and mental health, but not on women's empowerment.
					• There were large spillovers in the small village economies, including more women becoming traders, an increase in imports from major trading centers, and a fall in the consumer price index.
					• Close supervision and advising by the nongovernmental organization led to slight increases in economic success.
					• The rate of return calculated for the WINGS full package plus administration (using an increase in income of 6,200 Uganda Shillings per month for 15 years) was −33 percent when applying a discount rate of 15 percent for 15 years, +36 percent when applying a 3 percent discount rate for 15 years. Although the return of the intervention using the average income effect was positive at a lower discount rate, it was not possible to determine whether the inputs that went into the program were the most appropriate or optimal combination, versus their individual contribution to the outcome.

table continues next page

Entrepreneurship Training—Potential Entrepreneurs (ETPo)

Program name	Program beneficiaries	Evaluation	Sample	Outcomes measured	Key findings
YOP | Youth Opportunities Program | **Uganda** *Source:* Blattman, Fiala, and Martinez Forthcoming	Poor and under-employed youth ages 16 to 35 in Uganda's north	Randomized control trial	From the pool of 535 groups, 265 were randomly assigned to the intervention (treatment) and the remaining 279 to the control. The treatment and control youth were surveyed three times—at baseline and two and four years post-intervention.	Investment, occupational choice/levels, social issues and income	• The treatment group invested most of the grant in skills and business assets, and after four years they were 65 percent more likely to practice the skilled trade. • Earnings were 49 percent greater than the control group and 41 percent greater after four years. • The treatment group was more likely to engage in business practices such as keeping records, registering, and paying taxes. • There was a shift in occupational choice toward skilled work, where the treatment group was around 38 percent higher than the control, and it was larger for women. • Labor supply increased in response to the increase in capital for both men and women. • Earnings were larger for the treatment group and for both genders, but there was a catch-up by the control group after four years, primarily among men. • The wealth index was 0.2 standard deviation greater for the treated than for the control. • There was limited and weak evidence of a positive social impact after two years and none after four.

	Entrepreneurship Training—Practicing Entrepreneurs (ETPr)			
Program name	Program beneficiaries	Evaluation	Sample	Outcomes measured	Key findings

Program name	Program beneficiaries	Evaluation	Sample	Outcomes measured	Key findings
GNAG | Ghana National Association of Garages | **Ghana** Source: Mano et al. 2011	Approximately 1,000 metalwork entrepreneurs in the Suame Magazine, located in the city of Kumasi, Ghana	Randomized control trial	The pool of entrepreneurs was 167 metalwork entrepreneurs randomly selected from the GNAG member list. However, as a result of attrition and implementation problems, the final sample comprised 113 entrepreneurs. The treatment group had 47 entrepreneurs and the control had 66.	Adoption of practices and financial outcomes	• The training had a strong impact on the adoption of the recommended practices, although the firms experienced decreased profitability as a result of new competition. • After the training, the percentage of firms in the treatment group keeping records increased by 36 percentage points, whereas the increase was 6 percentage points in the control group. • Similarly, the percentage of firms in the treatment group analyzing business records increased by 34 percentage points, while the increase was about 3 percentage points in the control group. • However, these effects were not homogeneous, because between a third and half of participants did not adopt these practices. • The decrease in the sales and gross profits after the training were somewhat smaller for the treatment group than for the control group, respectively –12.9 percentage points compared with –19.6 for the sales, and –2.8 percentage points compared with –6.9 for the gross profits. Also, the effects of the training on the gross profits were much more significant than the effects of the training on sales revenues. • Participation in the training program increased the probability of survival by 8 or 9 percentage points.

table continues next page

Program name	Program beneficiaries	Evaluation	Sample	Outcomes measured	Key findings
MiDA- FBO| Millennium Development Authority—Farm-Based Organization Training| Ghana *Source:* Institute of Statistical, Social and Economic Research 2012	Farm-based organizations (FBOs) in 30 districts in the Northern Agricultural Zone, the Central African Basin Zone, and the Southern Horticultural Belt	Randomized phase-in approach	Approximately 1,200 FBOs were ex ante designed to be interviewed as part of the evaluation. Attrition rate was 10 percent.	Loans accessed and estimates on behavior (cultivated land size, chemical use and value, labor hours, and seed use)	• There was no evidence of intervention impact on crop yields and crop incomes overall, but there were significant zonal differences with crop incomes. • Training positively impacted the loan amounts that households received. • Training increased farmers' use of more formal sources for loans. • The intervention led to an increase in the use of improved seeds and fertilizers by farmers, but that was mainly driven by the starter pack that participants received.
PRIDE | PRIDE Microfinance | Tanzania *Source:* Bjorvatn and Tungodden 2010	The more than 300 clients of PRIDE microfinance in Dar es Salaam, Tanzania	Randomized control trial	A randomly selected subset was drawn from the pool of clients who were offered training. The sample size is 126 from the treated group and 126 from the control group. There was an attrition rate of 15 percent for the treatment and 13 percent for the control, but it did not affect the randomization. The final sample was 107 for the treatment and 104 for the control.	Participation and performance (the latter measured as entrepreneur business skills)	• The mean attendance for the sub-sample of the treated participants was 15.9 out of 21 sessions (76 percent), indicating that the training was perceived as beneficial for the businesses. • More schooled, more skilled (in terms of math), and more experienced (in terms of age) entrepreneurs had higher attendance than those who scored lower on these dimensions. The values of attendance were respectively 1.70 (significant at 10 percent), 1.62 (significant at 10 percent), and 2.26 (significant at 5 percent). • On average, the treatment group had a 9 percent higher score on the business knowledge test than the control group. • The effect of training appeared to be highest for entrepreneurs who participated frequently in the course, who initially did not have a lot of formal education but who did have strong cognitive skills.

table continues next page

Entrepreneurship Training—Practicing Entrepreneurs (ETPr)

Program name	Program beneficiaries	Evaluation	Sample	Outcomes measured	Key findings
WEP [Women Entrepreneurship Program] **South Africa** Source: Botha, Nieman, and van Vuuren 2006	Women who want to start their own business or have one and seek to improve their entrepreneurial and management skills.	Randomized control trial	New and established women entrepreneurs in South Africa. The evaluation had a treatment group of 116 women and a control group of 64 women.	Skills and knowledge on running a business, increase in number of employees, turnover, productivity, and profit	• There were statistically significant gains in the four skills transfer factors (entrepreneurial characteristics, entrepreneurial orientation, business knowledge, entrepreneurial and business skills) between treatment and control group. • There were statistically significant (at a 5 percent level) differences in effectiveness between treatment and control group in relation of business improvement factors. • There was improvement in the number of employees and the number of costumers for the treatment group (statistically significant), whereas this was not the case for the control group. • However, in business performance indicators (annual sales/turnover, value of capital assets, number of employees, number of customers per month, success of the businesses, probability of the businesses, satisfaction of the customers, and break-even point), both groups presented improvements before and after (mainly because of improvement in external factors of the economy). But they were statistically significant for the treatment group in 5 out of 6 indicators, while only 2 out of 6 indicators were statistically significant for the control group. • 98.12 percent of the treatment group were satisfied with WEP and indicated that they would recommend it to a friend or a colleague. • 96.94 percent of the experimental group stated that WEP had helped them grow their businesses and 97.96 percent indicated that WEP had some effect on their businesses six months after the training.

table continues next page

Entrepreneurship Training—Practicing Entrepreneurs (ETPr)

Program name	Program beneficiaries	Evaluation	Sample	Outcomes measured	Key findings
END |Endeavor| **South Africa** *Source:* IFC Monitor 2006	The target is mostly small and medium enterprises that are particularly conducive to innovation in South Africa	Quasi- experimental design	Sample size included a treatment group of 19 selected enterprises (EEs)—those who received the whole range of Endeavor's services—and a control group of 33 nonselected (non-EEs) applicants.	The effect of being chosen as a program participant on firms; total sales, export sales, number of employees, and income	• The program had positive effects on sales growth. • On average, sales for EEs increased by approximately USD\$193,000–USD\$290,000 more than non-EEs. • The effect on the percentage of export sales was not statistically significant; and • EEs' most used services were the mentoring, training course, and networking opportunities, but not all the services were used, showing that achieving all program objectives required some additional effort.
MSETTP | Micro and Small Enterprise Training and Technology Project | **Kenya** *Source:* World Bank 2005	The beneficiaries were the Jua Kali workers in the manufacturing sector. Nearly 32,000 MSE proprietors were trained between 1994 and 2002	Performance evaluation— beneficiaries (both trainees and trainers) were surveyed on the project's outcomes.	Running from 1994 to 2003, MSETTP also aimed to increase entrepreneurial development of the private sector, as well as increasing employment and incomes among informal-sector (Jua Kali) micro- and small-scale enterprises (MSEs).	• The tracer studies conducted showed that the program improved profits, sales and investment in a significant proportion of trainees, relative to a control group. It also encouraged business start-ups. • Nearly 35,000 MSEs received training, compared to the project's official target of 32,000. • Four out of five trainees reported that the relevance and quality of the training they received under the program was good or excellent. Trainees surveyed reported that thanks to the training they improved the quality of their product (43 percent), introduced a new product or service (71 percent), increased sales (66 percent), or found new markets (58 percent). A lower proportion (20 percent) reported that they enjoyed easier access to credit after receiving training. • The program encouraged some training providers to expand their training business (38 percent reported using their revenues to improve their training business), but the long-run impact of the project on markets for training services appeared to have been modest, as many trainers returned to their previous activities once the program ended. • The efficiency of the project was negligible mainly because of implementation problems.

table continues next page

TABLE: Entrepreneurship Training—Practicing Entrepreneurs (ETPr)

Program name	Program beneficiaries	Evaluation	Sample	Outcomes measured	Key findings
GOWE |Growth-Oriented Women Entrepreneurs| **Kenya** *Source:* ILO 2010	700 female entrepreneurs in Kenya	Qualitative insights from focus groups and one-on-one conversations among past participants.		The program aimed to improve participants' access to capital and mentorship and to enhance business knowledge and skills. Focused on female entrepreneurs in Kenya, the program involved (i) participants' access to finance at the African Development Bank, (ii) training and business mentorship, and (iii) improving the capacity of local business service providers to help with the delivery of services better targeted to beneficiaries.	• The trainings were highly rated by participants, but there was a common belief that the program needed better mentorship and experiential learning. • Past participants believed the program should have better follow-up around financing and should set training prices at market rates.

Source: World Bank.

a. A summary of this paper is available at http://www.nfte.com/sites/default/files/harvard-nfte_study_02-03_full_report_6-6-04.pdf. Full text is available upon request.

Bibliography

Acs, Z. J. 1992. "Small Business Economics: A Global Perspective." *Challenge* 35 (6): 38–44.

Acs, Z. J., and C. Armington. 2006. *Entrepreneurship, Geography, and American Economic Growth*. New York: Cambridge University Press.

Acs, Z. J., and A. Varga. 2005. "Entrepreneurship, Agglomeration and Technological Change." *Small Business Economics* 24 (3): 323–34.

African Economic Outlook. 2012. "Promoting Youth Employment." http://www. africaneconomicoutlook.org/en/in-depth/youth_employment/.

Altenburg, T. 2009. Presentation held at SolbjergPlads on 04/06/2009 DeutschesInstitutfürEntwicklungspolitik (DIE).

Aryeetey, E. 2001. "Human Capital Development for Socioeconomic Transformation." Ghana in the 21st Century ISSER Millennium Seminar Series, 8, Institute of Statistical, Social & Economic Research, University of Ghana.

Associação Industrial de Moçambique (AIMO). 2010. *Competitividade Industrial em Moçambique: Contribuição da AIMO*. Maputo: AIMO.

Associação Nacional das Empresas Metalúrgicas e Metalomecânicas (ANEMM). 2000. *Sectores de Destino da Produção da Metalurgia e Electromecânica, Moçambique*, Vol II. Lisboa: ANEMM.

Baiya, H., and J. Kithinji. 2010. *Transforming the Dairy Sector: Benefits from the Formalization of the Raw Milk Trade in Kenya*. SITE Case Study. Nairobi: SITE Enterprise Promotion.

Bandiera, O., R. Burgess, S. Guleschi, I. Rasul, and M. Suliman. 2012. "Can Entry-level Entrepreneurship Transform the Economic Lives of the Poor?" Paper originally presented at the Poverty and Applied Micro Seminar Series, World Bank, Washington, DC, March 21. Also available as a DfiD working paper at http://ipl.econ.duke.edu/ bread/papers/0413conf/bandiera.pdf.

Birch, D. 1979. *The Job Generation Process*. Cambridge, MA: MIT Program on Neighborhood and Regional Change.

Bjorvatn, K., and B. Tungodden. 2010. "Teaching Business in Tanzania: Evaluation Participation and Performance." *Journal of the European Economic Association* 8 (2–3): 61–570.

Blattman, C., N. Fiala, and S. Martinez. 2013. "Generating Skilled Self-Employment in Developing Countries: Experimental Evidence from Uganda." *Quarterly Journal of Economics*. http://papers.ssrn.com/sol3/papers.cfm?abstract_id=2268552.

Blattman, C., E. Green, J. Annan, and J. Jamison. 2013. "Building Women's Economic and Social Empowerment through Enterprise: An Experimental Assessment of the Women's Income Generating Support (WINGS) Program in Uganda." Published by enGender Impact, the World Bank's Gender Impact Evaluation Database. Retrieved from http://www.poverty-action.org/sites/default/files/wings_full_policy_report_0.pdf.

Bolstad, R. 2006. "Evaluation of the Northland Enterprising Teachers (NET) Initiative." New Zealand Council for Educational Research. http://www.nzcer.org.nz/pdfs/15059 .pdf.

Botha, M., G. H. Nieman, and J. J. van Vuuren. 2006. "Evaluating the Women Entrepreneurship Training Programme." *International Indigenous Journal of Entrepreneurship, Advancement, Strategy and Education* 2: 1–16.

Brock, W., and D. Evans. 1989. "Small Business Economics." *Small Business Economics* 1: 7–20.

Carree, M., and A. Thurik. 2003. "The Impact of Entrepreneurship on Economic Growth." In *Handbook of Entrepreneurship Research: An Interdisciplinary Survey and Introduction*, edited by Z. Acs and D. Audretsch. Boston: Kluwer Academic Publishers.

Charney, A., and K. E. Libecap. 2000. "The Impact of Entrepreneurship Education: An Evaluation of the Berger Entrepreneurship Program at the University of Arizona, 1985–1999." University of Arizona, Eller College of Business and Public Administration, Tucson, Arizona.

Cho, Y., and M. Honorati. 2013. "Entrepreneurship Programs in Developing Countries: A Meta-Regression Analysis." Social Protection and Labor Discussion Paper No. 1302, World Bank, Washington, DC.

Davidson, P., and J. Wiklund. 1997. "Values, Beliefs, and Regional Variations in New Firm Formation Rates." *Journal of Economic Psychology* 18 (2–3): 179–99.

De Mel, S., D. McKenzie, and C. Woodruff. 2009. "Measuring Microentrerprise Profits: Must We Ask How the Sausage Is Made?" *Journal of Development Economics* 88 (1): 19–31.

Dickson, P. H., G. T. Solomon, and K. M. Weaver. 2008. "Entrepreneurial Selection and Success: Does Education Matter?" *Journal of Small Business and Enterprise Development* 15: 239–58.

Fairlie, R. W., and A. M. Robb. 2007. "Families, Human Capital, and Small Business: Evidence from the Characteristics of Business Owners Survey." *Industrial and Labor Relations Review* 60: 225–45.

Farstard, H. 2002. *Integrated Entrepreneurship Education in Botswana, Uganda and Kenya.* Oslo: National Institute of Technology.

Filmer, D., L. Fox, K. Brooks, A. Goyal, T. Mengistae, P. Premand, D. Ringold, S. Sharma, and S. Zorya. 2014. *Youth Employment in Sub-Saharan Africa.* Washington, DC: World Bank.

Freedom House. 2008. "Political Freedom Index." http://www.freedomhouse.org.

Frese, M., and D. Zapf. 1994. "Action as the Core of Work Psychology: A German Approach." In *Handbook of Industrial and Organizational Psychology*, edited by H. C. Triandis, M. D. Dunnette, and J. M. Hough, Vol. 4, 2nd ed., 271–340. Palo Alto, CA: Consulting Psychology Press.

Fritsch, M. 2004. "Entrepreneurship, Entry and Performance of New Business Compared in Two Growth Regimes: East and West Germany." *Journal of Evolutionary Economics* 14: 525–42.

Ghana Statistical Service (GSS). 2013. Provisional Gross Domestic Product 2013.

Gielnik, M., M. Frese, A. Kahara-Kawuki, I. WassawaKatono, S. Kyejjusa, J. Munene, and T. J. Dlugosch. 2013. "Action and Action-Regulation in Entrepreneurship: Evaluating a

Student Training for Promoting Entrepreneurship." *Academy of ManagementLearning and Education*, October 3. http://amle.aom.org/content/early/2013/10/03/amle.2012.0107.abstract.

Glaub, M., and M. Frese. 2011. "A Critical Review of the Effects of Entrepreneurship Training in Developing Countries' Enterprise." *Development and Microfinance* 22 (4): 335–53.

Government of Kenya. 2008. "Medium Term Plan for Vision 2030 (2008–2012)." Nairobi.

———. 2009. "National Youth Council Act, No. 10 of 2009, Revised Edition 2012." http://kenyalaw.org/kl/fileadmin/pdfdownloads/Acts/NationalYouthCouncilAct_No10of2009.pdf.

———. 2012. "Economic Survey 2012." Nairobi.

Government of Mozambique. 2006. "Estratégia de Emprego e formação Profissional 2006–2015." www.portaldogoverno.gov.mz.docs_gov/estratégia/trabalho/estratégiadeemprego.pdf.

Hegarty, C. 2006. "It's Not an Exact Science: Teaching Entrepreneurship in Northern Ireland." *Education + Training* 48 (5): 322–35.

Heritage Foundation. 2008. "Index of Economic Freedom." Retrieved May 7, 2008, from http://www.heritage.org/research/features/index/downlads.cfm.

Hermes, N., and R. Lensink. 2007. "The Empirics of Microfinance: What Do We Know?" *Economic Journal* 117 (517):1–10.

Hofstede, G. 1991. *Cultures and Organizations: Software of the Mind*. Berkshire, UK: McGraw-Hill Book Company Europe.

Huber, L., R. Sloof, and M. V. van Praag. 2012. "The Effect of Early Entrepreneurship Education: Evidence from a Randomized Field Experiment." Discussion Paper 6512, Institute for the Study of Labour, Bonn.

Idogho, P. O., and A. E. Ainabor. 2011. "Entrepreneurship Education and Small-Scale Business Management Skill Development among Students of Auchi Polytechnic Auchi, Edo State, Nigeria." *International Journal of Business and Management* 6 (3): 284.

IFC Monitor. 2006. "Do Programs Supporting High Growth Entrepreneurs Work? Evaluating the Endeavor-South Africa Project." Monitor 45322, Endeavor Global, International Finance Corporation, and World Bank Group, Washington, DC.

Institute of Statistical, Social and Economic Research. 2012. "An Impact Evaluation of the MiDA FBO Training: Final Report." University of Ghana, Accra.

International Labour Organization (ILO). 2010. "ILO Evaluation Series: Growth-Oriented Women Entrepreneurs (GOWE)-Kenya Program." http://www.ilo.org/wcmsp5/groups/public/—ed_mas/—eval/documents/publication/wcms_142992.pdf.

———. 2011. "Building Business and Entrepreneurship Awareness: An ILO Experience of Integrating Entrepreneurship Education into National Vocational Education Systems." http://www.ilo.org/wcmsp5/groups/public/—ed_mas/—eval/documents/publication/wcms_142992.pdf.

———. 2013. *Key Indicators of Labor Markets*. 7th ed. http://kilm.ilo.org/manuscript/kilm13.asp.

———. 2014. "Global Employment Trends 2014." http://www.ilo.org/wcmsp5/groups/public/—dgreports/—dcomm/—publ/documents/publication/wcms_233953.pdf.

Isaacs, E., K. J. Visser, C. Friedrich, and P. Brijlal. 2007. "Entrepreneurship Education and Training at the Further Education and Training (FET) Level in South Africa." *South African Journal of Education* 27: 613–29.

Karlan, D., and M. Valdivia. 2011. "Teaching Entrepreneurship: Impact of Business Training on Microfinance Clients and Institutions." *Review of Economics and Statistics* 93 (2): 510–27.

Kenya National Bureau of Statistics (KNBS). 2007. "Basic Report on Well-being in Kenya." KNBS, Nairobi.

Lautenschläger, A., and H. Haase. 2011. "The Myth of Entrepreneurship Education: Seven Arguments Against Teaching Business Creation at Universities." *Journal of EntrepreneurshipEducation* 14: 147–61.

Lopes, M. 2006. *Os Empresários da Construção Civil e as Relações de Trabalho: Estratégias e Desafios, 1991–2004* (Construction Businesses and Labour Relations: Strategies and Challenges). Maputo: Faculdade de Economia, UEM.

Lüthje, C., and N. Franke. 2003. "The 'Making' of an Entrepreneur: Testing a Model of Entrepreneurial Intent Among Engineering Students at MIT." *R&D Management* 33 (2): 135–47.

Mahohoma, E., and M. Muyambo. 2008. "The Impact of Junior Achievement in Namibia." Junior Achievement Worldwide and Junior Achievement Namibia. http://www.docs toc.com/docs/51842795/JA-Namibia-Impact-Survey—REPOR.

Mano, Y., A. Iddrisu, Y. Yoshino, and S. Tetsushi. 2011. "How Can Micro and Small Enterprises in Sub-Saharan Africa Become More Productive? The Impacts of Experimental Basic Managerial Training." Policy Research Working Paper 5755, World Bank, Washington, DC.

Marrengula, C. P., V. Nhabinde, and U. Amosse. 2012. "The Challenges and the Way Forward for the Construction Industry in Mozambique." International Growth Centre. http://www.theigc.org/sites/default/files/Nhabine%20et%20al%202012%20 Mozambique%20Construction%20Working%20Paper.pdf.

Martin, B., J. J. McNally, and M. J. Kay. 2013. "Examining the Formation of Human Capital in Entrepreneurship: A Meta-Analysis of Entrepreneurship Education Outcomes." *Journal of Business Venturing* 28 (2): 211–24.

McKenzie, D., and C. Woodruff. 2012. "What Are We Learning from Business Training and Entrepreneurship Evaluations Around the Developing World?" Policy Research Working Paper 6202, World Bank, Washington, DC.

McKernan, S. M. 2002. "The Impact of Microcredit Programs on Self-Employment Profit: Do Non-Credit Program Aspects Matter?" *The Review of Economics and Statistics* 84 (1): 93–115.

Menzies, T. V. 2003. "21st Century Pragmatism: Universities and Entrepreneurship Education and Development." Keynote Address presented at the ICSB World Conference, Belfast, Northern Ireland.

Monitor Consulting Group. 2012. "Accelerating Entrepreneurship in Africa: Understanding Africa's Challenges to Creating Opportunity-Driven Entrepreneurship." Monitor Group and the Omidyar Network. Retrieved from http://www.omidyar.com/sites/ default/files/file/ON%20Africa%20Report_April%202013_FInal.pdf.

Mwasalwiba, E. S. 2010. "Entrepreneurship Education: A Review of its Objectives, Teaching Methods, and Impact Indicators." *Education + Training* 52 (1): 20–47.

Nakkula, M., M. Lutyens, C. Pineda, A. Dray, F. Gaytan, and J. Huguley. 2004. "Initiating, Leading and Feeling in Control of One's Fate: Findings from the 2002–2003 Study of NFTE in Six Boston Public High Schools." Harvard University. http://www.nfte.com/sites/default/files/harvard-nfte_study_02-03_full_report_6-6-04.pdf.

NKC Independent Economists. 2012. "Mozambique Country Profile." http://www.nkc.co.za/?NKC/99:0:0:0/Mozambique.html.

Osei-Boateng, C., and E. Ampratwum. 2011. "The Informal Sector in Ghana." Friedricch Ebert Stiftung. www.fesghana.org/uploads/PDF/FES_InformalSector_2011_FINAL.pdf.

Paulson, A. L., and R. Townsend. 2004. "Entrepreneurship and Financial Constraints in Thailand." *Journal of Corporate Finance* 10: 229–36.

Pinillos, M.-J., and L. Reyes. 2011. "Relationship Between Individualist-Collectivist Culture and Entrepreneurial Activity: Evidence From Global Entrepreneurship Monitor Data." *Small Business Economics* 37: 23–37.

Pittaway, L., and J. Cope. 2007. "Entrepreneurship Education: A Systematic Review of the Evidence." *International Small Business Journal* 25 (5): 477–506.

Rauch, A., and M. Frese. 2007. "Let's Put the Person Back Into Entrepreneurship Research: A Meta-Analysis on the Relationship Between Business Owners' Personality Traits, Business Creation and Success." *European Journal of Work and Organizational Psychology* 16 (4): 353–85.

Rauch, A., M. Frese, and S. Sonnentag. 2000. "Cultural Differences in Planning/Success Relationships: A Comparison of Small Enterprises in Ireland, West Germany, and East Germany." *Journal of Small Business Management* 38: 28–41.

Reimers, F., P. Dyer, and M. E. Ortega. 2012. "Entrepreneurship Education in the Middle East." https://www.jaworldwide.org/inside-ja/Reports/INJAZ_Al_Arab_Final_Evaluation_Report.pdf.

Schramm, C., and R. Litan. 2009. "Up from Poverty." *Real Clear Markets*. Retrieved August 30, 2013, from http://www.realclearmarkets.com/articles/2009/05/up_from_poverty.html.

Souitaris, V., S. Zerbinati, and A. Al-Laham. 2007. "Do Entrepreneurship Programmes Raise Entrepreneurial Intentions of Science and Engineering Students." *Journal of Business Venturing* 22: 566–91.

South African Institute for Entrepreneurship. 2006. "Business Ventures Full Impact Report." Retrieved August 8, 2013, from http://www.entrepreneurship.co.za/page/business_ventures_full_impact_report.

Unger, J. M., A. Rauch, M. Frese, and N. Rosenbusch. 2011. "Human Capital and Entrepreneurial Success: A Meta-Analytical Review." *Journal of Business Venturing* 26: 341–58.

United Nations Development Program. 2013. "Kenya's Youth Employment Challenge." Discussion Paper, United Nations Development Program, New York.

Valerio, A., B. Parton, and A. Robb. 2014. *Entrepreneurship Education and Training Around the World: Dimensions for Success*. Washington, DC: World Bank.

Van der Sluis, J., M. van Praag, and W. Vijverberg. 2008. "Education and Entrepreneurship Selection and Performance: A Review of Empirical Literature." *Journal of Economic Surveys* 22 (5): 795–841. doi: 10.1111/j.1467-6419.2008.00550.X.

Van Praag, M., and P. H. Versloot. 2007. "What Is the Value of Entrepreneurship? A Review of Recent Research." *Small Business Economics* 29: 351–82.

Volkmann, C. 2009. "Entrepreneurship in Higher Education." In *Educating the Next Wave of Entrepreneurs: Unlocking Entrepreneurial Capabilities to Meet the Global Challenges of the 21st Century*, edited by C. Volkmann, K. E. Wilson, S. Mariotti, D. Rabuzzi, S. Vyakarnam, and A. Sepulveda. Cologny/Geneva: World Economic Forum.

Walter, S., and D. Dohse. 2009. *The Interplay Between Entrepreneurship Education and Regional Knowledge Potential in Forming Entrepreneurial Intentions*. Kiel, Germany: Kiel Institute for the World Economy.

World Bank. 2005. "Project Performance Assessment Report: Kenya Micro and Small Enterprise Training and Technology Project." Report 32657, Washington, DC.

———. 2010a. *Stepping Up Skills: For More Jobs and Higher Productivity*. Washington, DC: World Bank.

———. 2010b. *Country Partnership Strategy for the Republic of Kenya for the Period FY2010-13*. Washington, DC: World Bank.

———. 2011a. "Doing Business 2010 Mozambique." Washington, DC.

———. 2011b. *Learning for All: Investing in People's Knowledge and Skills to Promote Development*. Washington, DC: World Bank.

———. 2012a. "Energizing Kenya's Economy and Creating Quality Jobs." Kenya Economic Update, World Bank, Washington, DC, December.

———. 2012b. *Resilience, Equity and Opportunity: Social Protection and Labor Strategy 2012–2020*. Washington, DC: World Bank.

———. 2012c. "Walking on a Tightrope—Rebalancing Kenya's Economy With Special Emphasis on Regional Integration." Kenya Economic Update, World Bank, Washington, DC, June.

———. 2012d. *World Development Report 2013: Jobs*. Washington, DC: World Bank.

———. 2012e. *Can Skills Training Programs Increase Employment for Young Women? The Case of Liberia*. Washington, DC: Adolescent Girls Initiative, World Bank.

———. 2012f. *Country Partnership Strategy for the Republic of Mozambique for the Period FY2013–16*. Washington, DC: World Bank.

———. 2013a. *Doing Business 2013*. Washington, DC: World Bank. www.doingbusiness.org.

———. 2013b. *Country Partnership Strategy for the Republic of Ghana for the Period FY2013–16*. Washington, DC: World Bank.

———. 2013c. *Reinvigorating Growth with a Dynamic Banking Sector*. Kenya Economic Update, December. Washington, DC: World Bank.

Environmental Benefits Statement

The World Bank is committed to reducing its environmental footprint. In support of this commitment, the Publishing and Knowledge Division leverages electronic publishing options and print-on-demand technology, which is located in regional hubs worldwide. Together, these initiatives enable print runs to be lowered and shipping distances decreased, resulting in reduced paper consumption, chemical use, greenhouse gas emissions, and waste.

The Publishing and Knowledge Division follows the recommended standards for paper use set by the Green Press Initiative. Whenever possible, books are printed on 50 percent to 100 percent postconsumer recycled paper, and at least 50 percent of the fiber in our book paper is either unbleached or bleached using Totally Chlorine Free (TCF), Processed Chlorine Free (PCF), or Enhanced Elemental Chlorine Free (EECF) processes.

More information about the Bank's environmental philosophy can be found at http://crinfo.worldbank.org/wbcrinfo/node/4.

green press INITIATIVE

www.ingramcontent.com/pod-product-compliance
Lightning Source LLC
Chambersburg PA
CBHW082103210326
41599CB00033B/6571